THE ENGINEER OF 2020

VISIONS OF ENGINEERING
IN THE NEW CENTURY

NATIONAL ACADEMY OF ENGINEERING
OF THE NATIONAL ACADEMIES

THE NATIONAL ACADEMIES PRESS
Washington, DC
www.nap.edu

THE NATIONAL ACADEMIES PRESS   500 Fifth Street, N.W.   Washington, DC 20001

Funding for the activity that led to this publication was provided by the National Science Foundation, NEC Foundation of America, SBC Foundation, and Honeywell International, and the National Academy of Engineering Fund.

International Standard Book Number 0-309-09162-4 (Book)
International Standard Book Number 0-309-53065-2 (PDF)

Copies of this report are available from the National Academies Press, 500 Fifth Street, N.W., Lockbox 285, Washington, D.C. 20055; (800) 624-6242 or (202) 334-3313 (in the Washington metropolitan area); online at http://www.nap.edu.

THE NATIONAL ACADEMIES
Advisers to the Nation on Science, Engineering, and Medicine

The **National Academy of Sciences** is a private, nonprofit, self-perpetuating society of distinguished scholars engaged in scientific and engineering research, dedicated to the furtherance of science and technology and to their use for the general welfare. Upon the authority of the charter granted to it by the Congress in 1863, the Academy has a mandate that requires it to advise the federal government on scientific and technical matters. Dr. Bruce M. Alberts is president of the National Academy of Sciences.

The **National Academy of Engineering** was established in 1964, under the charter of the National Academy of Sciences, as a parallel organization of outstanding engineers. It is autonomous in its administration and in the selection of its members, sharing with the National Academy of Sciences the responsibility for advising the federal government. The National Academy of Engineering also sponsors engineering programs aimed at meeting national needs, encourages education and research, and recognizes the superior achievements of engineers. Dr. Wm. A. Wulf is president of the National Academy of Engineering.

The **Institute of Medicine** was established in 1970 by the National Academy of Sciences to secure the services of eminent members of appropriate professions in the examination of policy matters pertaining to the health of the public. The Institute acts under the responsibility given to the National Academy of Sciences by its congressional charter to be an adviser to the federal government and, upon its own initiative, to identify issues of medical care, research, and education. Dr. Harvey V. Fineberg is president of the Institute of Medicine.

The **National Research Council** was organized by the National Academy of Sciences in 1916 to associate the broad community of science and technology with the Academy's purposes of furthering knowledge and advising the federal government. Functioning in accordance with general policies determined by the Academy, the Council has become the principal operating agency of both the National Academy of Sciences and the National Academy of Engineering in providing services to the government, the public, and the scientific and engineering communities. The Council is administered jointly by both Academies and the Institute of Medicine. Dr. Bruce M. Alberts and Dr. Wm. A. Wulf are chair and vice chair, respectively, of the National Research Council.

www.national-academies.org

Acknowledgments

About Honeywell International

Honeywell is a diversified technology and manufacturing leader of aerospace products and services; control technologies for buildings, homes, and industry; automotive products; power generation systems; specialty chemicals; fibers; plastics and advanced materials. The company is committed to providing quality products, integrated system solutions, and services to customers around the world. Honeywell products touch the lives of most people everyday. The company's philanthropic giving is overseen by the Honeywell International Foundation. The Foundation is currently focused in three strategic areas: Family Safety and Security, Housing and Shelter, and Science and Math Education.

About NEC Foundation of America

NEC Foundation of America was established in 1991 and endowed at $10 million by NEC and its United States subsidiaries. Income generated by the endowment is donated to nonprofit organizations in the United States to help assure that individuals have the skills to advance the boundaries of technology, and to be served by innovation on both a personal and societal level. As of March 1, 2003, the Foundation's sole focus is technology for people with disabilities.

About National Science Foundation

The National Science Foundation (NSF) was established in 1950 by the Congress and is the only federal agency dedicated to supporting education and fundamental research in all science and engineering disciplines. The mission of NSF is to ensure that the United States maintains leadership in scientific discovery and the development of new technologies. NSF promotes the progress of engineering in the United States in order to enable the nation's capacity for innovation and to support the creation of wealth and a better quality of life.

About SBC Foundation

SBC Foundation is committed to supporting programs and organizations that promote the importance of a K-16 education continuum. Since its formation in 1984, SBC Foundation has distributed more than $203 million to fund educational endeavors across the United States. SBC Foundation-backed programs are designed to increase access to information technologies, broaden technology training and professional skills development, and integrate new technologies to enhance education and economic development. The Foundation is an independent entity and receives all of its funding from SBC Communications, Inc. and its family of companies.

COMMITTEE ON THE ENGINEER OF 2020

G. WAYNE CLOUGH (NAE), *Chair*, Georgia Institute of Technology
ALICE M. AGOGINO (NAE), University of California, Berkeley
GEORGE CAMPBELL, JR., The Cooper Union for the Advancement
    of Science and Art
JAMES CHAVEZ, Sandia National Laboratories
DAVID O. CRAIG, Reliant Energy
JOSÉ B. CRUZ, JR. (NAE), Ohio State University
PEGGY GIRSHMAN, National Public Radio
DANIEL E. HASTINGS, Massachusetts Institute of Technology
MICHAEL J. HELLER, University of California, San Diego
DEBORAH G. JOHNSON, University of Virginia
ALAN C. KAY (NAE), Hewlett-Packard Company
TAREK M. KHALIL, University of Miami
ROBERT W. LUCKY (NAE), Telcordia Technologies
JOHN M. MULVEY, Princeton University
SHARON L. NUNES, International Business Machines, Inc.
HENRY PETROSKI (NAE), Duke University
SUE V. ROSSER, Georgia Institute of Technology
ERNEST T. SMERDON (NAE), University of Arizona

PROJECT LIAISON

STEPHEN W. DIRECTOR (NAE), University of Michigan

NAE PROGRAM OFFICE STAFF

PATRICIA F. MEAD, Study Director
JORDAN J. BARUCH, Fellow
MATTHEW CAIA, Project Assistant (through March 2003)
LANCE DAVIS, Executive Officer and Acting Director, Program Office
ELIZABETH HOLLENBECK, Intern
NATHAN KAHL, Project Assistant
JAMIE OSTROHA, Intern
ERICKA REID, Intern
PROCTOR REID, Associate Director, Program Office

COMMITTEE ON ENGINEERING EDUCATION

STEPHEN W. DIRECTOR (NAE), *Chair*, University of Michigan
ALICE M. AGOGINO (NAE), University of California, Berkeley
ANJAN BOSE (NAE), Washington State University
ANTHONY BRIGHT, Harvey Mudd College
BARRY C. BUCKLAND (NAE), Merck Research Laboratories
G. WAYNE CLOUGH (NAE), Georgia Institute of Technology
MICHAEL CORRADINI (NAE), University of Wisconsin, Madison
JENNIFER SINCLAIR CURTIS, Purdue University
RODNEY CUSTER, Illinois State University
JAMES W. DALLY (NAE), University of Maryland, College Park
RUTH A. DAVID (NAE), ANSER Corporation
ANN Q. GATES, University of Texas, El Paso
RANDY HINRICHS, Microsoft Corporation
ROSALYN HOBSON, Virginia Commonwealth University
BARRY C. JOHNSON (NAE), Villanova University
LARRY V. McINTIRE (NAE), Rice University

EX OFFICIO MEMBERS

BRUCE ALBERTS (NAS), President, National Academy of Sciences
HARVEY FINEBERG (IOM), President, Institute of Medicine
GEORGE M.C. FISHER (NAE), Chairman, National Academy of
    Engineering
SHEILA E. WIDNALL (NAE), Vice President, National Academy of
    Engineering
WM. A. WULF (NAE), President, National Academy of Engineering

REVIEW COMMITEE

This report was reviewed by individuals chosen for their diverse perspectives and technical expertise, in accordance with procedures approved by the National Academies. The purpose of this independent review is to provide candid and critical comments that will assist the authoring committee and the NAE in making the published report as sound as possible and to ensure that the report meets institutional standards for objectivity, evidence, and responsiveness to the charge for this activity. The contents of the review comments and draft manuscript remain confidential to protect the integrity of the deliberative process.

JOHN A. ALIC, Consultant
DAVID P. BILLINGTON, Princeton University
JAMES J. DUDERSTADT, University of Michigan
SHERRA E. KERNS, Olin College
BINDU N. LAHANI, Asian Development Bank
EDWARD D. LAZOWSKA, University of Washington
IOANNIS N. MIAOULIS, Boston Museum of Science
CHERRY A. MURRAY, Lucent Technologies
ROBERT M. NEREM, Georgia Institute of Technology
SHERI SHEPPARD, Stanford University

REPORT REVIEW MONITOR

C. DAN MOTE, JR., University of Maryland, College Park

Preface

The Engineer of 2020 Project centers on an effort to envision the future and to use that knowledge to attempt to predict the roles that engineers will play in the future. While of interest in itself, the exercise is also intended to provide a framework that will be used in subsequent work to position engineering education in the United States for what lies ahead, rather than waiting for time to pass and then trying to respond. This initiative is not unique in that other groups have somewhat similar efforts under way or have recently completed them. The work of the National Academy of Engineering (NAE) differs in that it considers the issues with respect to all the diverse branches of engineering and examines them from the broadest possible perspective. Its principal focus is on the future of undergraduate engineering education in this country, although it is appreciated that to understand the full perspective engineering practice and engineering education must be considered in a global context.

Originated and chartered by the NAE's Committee on Engineering Education, the project consists of two parts, the first relating to the development of a vision for engineering and the work of the engineer in 2020. This phase of the work culminates with this report. The second part, which is yet to be completed, is to examine engineering education and ask what it needs to do to prepare engineers for the future. This report will be used to frame the discussions of the second phase.

A steering committee for the project was established in December 2001 by the NAE president to guide the work. The committee met four times over the course of the following year and developed a plan for a three-day workshop on the future of engineering that was held in Woods Hole, Massachusetts, in fall 2002. Thirty-five participants took part in the workshop representing a range of different disciplines, age groups, and points of view (see Appendix B). Keynote addresses were given by Phil Condit, Bran Ferren, and Shirley Ann Jackson.

At the outset it was agreed that predicting the future with any exactitude is not possible. Hence, scenario-based strategic planning was used to help the participants think broadly about events and issues that could shape the future. Peter Schwartz, a well-known author and strategic planning consultant, served as moderator and facilitator. During the course of the workshop, four scenarios were considered, each of which was thought to capture trends that could dramatically affect the way the future would unfold. All of the scenarios recognized that pending breakthroughs in technology from fields like nanotechnology, biotechnology, materials, computing, and logistics would be factors engendering change regardless of other conditions. It was understood that 2020 might reflect any one of the scenarios, some combination of them, or none of them. Their purpose was primarily realized through the process, which helped expand our appreciation of possibilities for the future and assisted in thinking about the future of engineering in these terms. The scenarios examine transformational changes that could derive from life-altering developments across several technological fronts, dramatic breakthroughs in biotechnology, a major natural disaster, and world division driven by growth in religious fundamentalism.

After the workshop, members of the steering committee were assigned the task of writing the report. A final meeting of the committee was held in December 2002 to critique the work of the writing groups. The final draft report was informed using the workshop keynote presentations, discussions, and scenarios as well as a steering committee consensus about new technologies that are likely to significantly influence the future course of engineering. Following the last meeting, a smaller group of the steering committee took on the task of editing the report for publication.

It is notable that this report posits a statement of aspirations for the engineer of 2020 and closes with a statement of attributes thought suitable for the engineer of 2020 that match the aspirations. The final two chapters express a bold optimism for the engineering profession if it is willing to confront the possibilities for the future and prepare for it.

Ahead lies the challenge of considering what engineering students should learn in the university to prepare for the future and how this might differ from what is taught today. This effort will take place over the course of the coming year through a new workshop and continuing work of the steering committee.

Contents

Executive Summary

In the past, changes in the engineering profession and engineering education have followed changes in technology and society. Disciplines were added and curricula were created to meet the critical challenges in society and to provide the workforce required to integrate new developments into our economy. Today's landscape is little different; society continually changes and engineering must adapt to remain relevant. But we must ask if it serves the nation well to permit the engineering profession and engineering education to lag technology and society, especially as technological change occurs at a faster and faster pace. Rather, should the engineering profession anticipate needed advances and prepare for a future where it will provide more benefit to humankind? Likewise, should engineering education evolve to do the same?

Technology has shifted the societal framework by lengthening our life spans, enabling people to communicate in ways unimaginable in the past, and creating wealth and economic growth by bringing the virtues of innovation and enhanced functionality to the economy in ever-shorter product development cycles. Even more remarkable opportunities are fast approaching through new developments in nanotechnology, logistics, biotechnology, and high-performance computing. At the same time, with tightening global linkages, new challenges and opportunities are emerging as a consequence of rapidly improving technological capabilities in such nations as India and China and the threat of terrorism around the world.

This report is the result of an initiative of the National Academy of Engineering that attempts to prepare for the future of engineering by asking the question, "What will or should engineering be like in 2020?" Will it be a reflection of the engineering of today and its past growth patterns or will it be fundamentally different? Most importantly, can the engineering profession play a role in shaping its own future? Can a future be created where engineering has a broadly recognized image that celebrates the exciting roles that engineering and engineers play in addressing societal and technical challenges? How can engineers best be educated to be leaders, able to balance the gains afforded by new technologies with the vulnerabilities created by their byproducts without compromising the well-being of society and humanity? Will engineering be viewed as a foundation that prepares citizens for a broad range of creative career opportunities? Will engineering reflect and celebrate the diversity of all the citizens in our society? Whatever the answers to these questions, without doubt, difficult problems and opportunities lie ahead that will call for engineering solutions and the talents of a creative engineering mind-set.

Because precise predictions of the future are difficult at best, the committee approached its charge using the technique of scenario-based planning. The benefit of the scenario approach was that it eliminated the need to develop a consensus view of a single future and opened thinking to include multiple possibilities. This technique has proven its worth for private and public entities alike in helping devise flexible strategies that can adapt to changing conditions. Specific scenarios considered in this project were (1) The Next Scientific Revolution, (2) The Biotechnology Revolution in a Societal Context, (3) The Natural World Interrupts the Technology Cycle, and (4) Global Conflict or Globalization? The story form of each scenario is presented in Appendix A. These sometimes colorful versions only partially capture the vigorous discussions and debates that took place, but they serve to illustrate and document the thinking involved in the process. Each in its own way informed the deliberations about possibilities that can shape the role that engineering will play in the future.

The "next scientific revolution" scenario offers an optimistic future where change is principally driven by developments in technology. It is assumed that the future will follow a predictable path where technologies that are on the horizon today are developed to a state where they can be used in commercial applications and their role is optimized to the benefit of society. As in the past, engineers will exploit new science to develop technologies that benefit humankind, and in others they will create new technologies de novo that demand new science to fully understand them. The importance of technology continues to grow in society as new developments are commercialized and implemented.

The "biotechnology revolution" scenario speaks to a specific area of science and engineering that holds great potential but considers a perspective where political and societal implications could intervene in its use. In this version of the future, issues that impact technological change beyond the scope of engineering become significant, as seen in the current debate over the use of transgenic foods. While the role of engineering is still of prime importance, the impact of societal attitudes and politics reminds us that the ultimate use of a new technology and the pace of its adoption are not always a simple matter.

The "natural world" scenario recognizes that events originating beyond man's control, such as natural disasters, can still be a determinate in the future. While in this case the role of future engineers and new technologies will be important to speeding a recovery from a disastrous event, it also can help in improving our ability to predict risk and adapt systems to prepare for the possibilities to minimize impact. For example, there is the likely possibility that computational power will improve such that accurate long-range weather predictions will be possible for relatively small geographic areas. This will allow defensive designs to be developed and customized for local conditions.

The final scenario examines the influence of global changes, as these can impact the future through conflict or, more broadly, through globalization. Engineering is particularly sensitive to such issues because it speaks through an international language of mathematics, science, and technology. Today's environment, with issues related to terrorism and job outsourcing, illustrates why this scenario is useful to consider in planning for the future.

The body of the report begins in Chapter 1 with a review designed to set the stage for likely future technological changes and challenges that will impact the world and the engineering profession. Dramatic expansion of knowledge is expected that will offer exciting opportunities for engineering to develop new technologies to address the problems faced by society. The impact will be seen in medical breakthroughs, new energy devices, materials with characteristics not available today, remarkable light sources, and next-generation computers and telecommunications developments. Engineering has contributed enormously to the quality of life we enjoy today, and the opportunities for the future are likely to be ever greater. The challenges include, among others, deteriorating infrastructure, environmental issues, and providing housing, water, and health care for a rapidly growing population.

Chapter 2 addresses the societal, geopolitical, and professional contexts within which engineering and its new technologies will exist. The coming era will be characterized by rapid population growth, which will contain internal dynamics that affect the types of problems engineers will face as well as world stability. Growth will be concentrated in less developed countries where a "youth bulge" will occur, while in advanced countries the population will age. Issues related to quality of life in some countries will be contrasted with more basic problems like access to water and housing in others. Within countries the demographics will change, particularly in the United States, where the numbers of minorities will grow rapidly while those of the traditional majority will decline in a relative sense. This has major implications for the future of engineering, a profession where minorities and women remain underrepresented.

While certain basics of engineering will not change, the global economy and the way engineers will work will reflect an ongoing evolution that began to gain momentum a decade ago. The economy in which we will work will be strongly influenced by the global marketplace for engineering services, a growing need for interdisciplinary and system-based approaches, demands for customerization, and an increasingly diverse talent pool. The steady integration of technology in our infrastructure and lives calls for more involvement by engineers in the setting of public policy and in participation in the civic arena. The external forces in society, the economy, and the professional environment pose imperatives for change that may exceed those to come from the changes expected in the technology engineers will have at their disposal in 2020. Challenges will abound, but opportunities also will exist if engineering takes the initiative to prepare for the future.

Chapter 3 builds on the context of the earlier chapters with a statement of aspirations for engineering in 2020. Its purpose is to identify those basic themes we can agree are worth striving for if engineering is to be a positive force in the future. The range of possibilities as contrasted with the realities makes this no easy task. As illustrated by the scenarios, they can be constrained by outside forces as well as by our own inaction. The aspirations chosen set the bar high but are believed to be attainable if a course of action is set to reach them. At their core they call for us to educate engineers who are broadly educated, who see themselves as global citizens, who can be leaders in business and public service, and who are ethically grounded.

Chapter 4 takes the aspirations a step further by setting forth the attributes needed for the graduates of 2020. These include such traits as strong analytical skills, creativity, ingenuity, professionalism, and leadership.

This study suggests that if the engineering profession is to take the initiative in defining its own future, it must (1) agree on an exciting vision for its future; (2) transform engineering education to help achieve the vision; (3) build a clear image of the new roles for engineers, including as broad-based technology leaders, in the mind of the public and prospective students who can replenish and improve the talent base of an aging engineering workforce; (4) accommodate innovative developments from nonengineering fields; and (5) find ways to focus the energies of the different disciplines of engineering toward common goals.

If the United States is to maintain its economic leadership and be able to sustain its share of high-technology jobs, it must prepare for a new wave of change. While there is no consensus at this stage, it is agreed that innovation is the key and engineering is essential to this task; but engineering will only contribute to success if it is able to continue to adapt to new trends and educate the next generation of students so as to arm them with the tools needed for the world as it will be, not as it is today.

1

Technological Context of Engineering Practice

TECHNOLOGICAL CHANGE

Engineering is a profoundly creative process. A most elegant description is that engineering is about design under constraint. The engineer designs devices, components, subsystems, and systems and, to create a successful design, in the sense that it leads directly or indirectly to an improvement in our quality of life, must work within the constraints provided by technical, economic, business, political, social, and ethical issues. Technology is the outcome of engineering; it is rare that science translates directly to technology, just as it is not true that engineering is just applied science. Historically, technological advances, such as the airplane, steam engine, and internal combustion engine, have occurred before the underlying science was developed to explain how they work. Yet, of course, when such explanations were forthcoming, they helped drive refinements that made the technology more valuable still.

Technological innovations occur when a need arises or an opportunity presents itself. They occur as a result of private initiative or government intervention. Most important for this study is that they are occurring at an astonishing pace, especially those in information and communications technology, which are most apparent to the public, and this has important implications for engineering practice and engineering education in the future. Totally unexpected scientific findings can suggest new technologies as well, and hence any discussion of the future of engineering must ponder scientific breakthroughs that might occur along the way.

In his groundbreaking book *The Structure of Scientific Revolutions,* Thomas Kuhn (1970) helped us see that science advances through two quite different dynamics. Ordinary science fills in the details of a landscape that is largely known. Every once in a while the problems of the contemporary world view become so unworkable that reinventing the map is needed. For example, the recognition that continents moved slowly over the surface of the earth solved many problems that a model of a static planet made unsolvable. This recognition led to a reconceptualization and new perception of reality.

One of the questions our view of the world answers is how things are connected and put together. The familiar model is a building constructed of diverse components assembled in a fixed pattern. The other familiar model is a fluid, like a river, with a rapidly changing shape formed by local conditions. An emerging model of order is the network. In a universe of superstrings and soft boundaries for molecules, network-like connections among things may provide a useful new ordering principle. Networks have unique properties, such as self-organization, and sometimes huge multiplier effects of many connecting to many. Networks also have vulnerabilities, as demonstrated by the blackout in the northeastern United States in August 2003.

We are also seeing a new relationship between the macroscopic world we inhabit every day and the microscopic world at a molecular, atomic, and even subatomic level. Once we could describe events in our observable world by fairly simple mathematical rules, say the trajectory of a baseball hit out of a baseball park, but the very small was imprecise, uncertain, and statistical. Now new tools and mathematics enable us to enjoy a similar level of precision, certainty, and uniqueness even at the smallest imaginable scales. We have, for example, recently discovered how to encode data in the spin of an electron inside an atom—in other words, subatomic data storage (Awschalom et al., 2002).

Both the exquisite sensitivity of biological function to the precise sequencing of base pairs of DNA and the mathematics of chaos lead to a view that small actions matter in giving form to things and order to events. What we do actually matters to history. The future really is the result of choices made today. It is not merely the random concatenation of mechanically predetermined events or the statistical result of accidents along the way. And while we are alike in many ways that define our common humanity, the path dependence of complex systems tells us that each of us is also unique.

In the old world view it took a builder to make a machine. Someone outside with a plan and the ability to assemble the parts is needed to get to a new machine. In the new world view, self-replication is a new model of change. In biology, self-replication is the norm, whether by simple mechanisms like cell division or more complex sexual methods. Now in nanotechnology and potentially in very smart computer systems, we are beginning to contemplate self-replication in nonorganic systems, and, indeed, runaway self-replication is seen as a threat by some.

The universe, as now understood, is vastly different than both the one Newton described and the one we "knew" as little as 50 years ago. Soon our world view may be distinct from that of Einstein and Bohr. Yet in this dynamic and confusing milieu, it is not clear which technical trends will move forward in a predictable fashion and which will burst forward as a revolution, forcing us to reconceptualize and reperceive our view of engineering. It is a daunting challenge for the engineering profession and engineering education to remain flexible enough to anticipate such changes or, if anticipation fails, to respond as rapidly as possible.

Change is constant, but on an absolute basis our world has changed more in the past 100 years than in all those preceding. By the end of the 20th century, the developed world had become a healthier, safer, and more productive place; a place where engineering, through technology, had forged an irreversible imprint on our lives and our identity. The Swiss engineer Jurgen Mittelstrass once termed the present technology-dominated world as the "Leonardoworld," to contrast with the time long past where human life was dominated by the natural world (Mittelstrass, 2001). There are many positive aspects of this new world—longer and healthier lives, improved work and living conditions, global communications, ease of transit, and access to art and culture—and this is true for the masses in the developed world instead of only a privileged few. Making it true for the masses in the developing world is one of the great moral and ethical challenges for society as a whole but for engineers in particular.

Looking forward to further changes in science and technology, perhaps revolutionary changes, we are limited by our inability to see the future, but our imagination is reflected in the scenarios in Appendix A.

Turning to reality, though, the best we can do is look at recent and emergent advances, like those in biotechnology, nanotechnology, information and communications technology, materials science, and photonics to provide a possible template of the changes engineering will need to contend with in 2020.

BREAKTHROUGH TECHNOLOGIES

Biotechnology

Exciting breakthroughs in our understanding of human physiology have been among the most captivating topics of public discussion over the past several decades. It is the potential to attack diseases and disorders at the cell and DNA levels that leads some to believe that diseases, as currently known, may be eradicated and that compensations for many of the limitations of the human body (e.g., those related to aging or hormonal changes) will be available.

Advances in biotechnology have already significantly improved the quality of our lives, but even more dramatic breakthroughs are likely. Research in tissue engineering and regenerative medicine may lead to new technology that will allow our bodies to replace injured or diseased parts without invasive surgery, but rather by using the natural growth processes inherent in cells. Already used extensively to help burn victims grow replacement skin, it is possible that related developments will allow spinal cord injury victims to restore full mobility and feeling by reconnecting tissues and nerves.

Linked with new developments in nanotechnology and micro-electronic mechanical systems (MEMS), we may see the use of nanoscale robots, or nanobots, to repair tissue tears or clean clogged arteries. Nanobots might be used to target drugs that can destroy cancers or change cell structures to combat genetically inherited diseases. Bioinformatics will likely take advantage of improved computing capabilities that use the human genome database to allow drugs to be customized for each individual. A drug that might be fatal for one person could be well suited for curing another's disease, depending on their specific genetic makeup.

The intersection of medical knowledge and engineering has spawned new biomedical engineering research and curricula that have helped create or refine products such as pacemakers, artificial organs, prosthetic devices, laser eye surgery, an array of sophisticated imaging systems, and fiber-optic-assisted noninvasive surgical techniques. In the future, ongoing developments will expand beyond the application of medical advances toward tighter connections between technology and the human experience. For example, embedded devices that aid communication or devices that monitor organ functions and provide meaningful information to the user will be available. New-century products will also be exquisitely tailored to match the physical dimensions and capabilities of the user. Bio-inspired computer researchers are already investigating virus protection architectures that mimic the human viral defense system, and pattern recognition researchers are developing algorithms that mimic the visioning processes observed in humans and other species (National Research Council, 2001). Ergonomic design and an eye on other physical and mental health influences of engineered products will be an underlying theme across all engineering disciplines.

There are already engineers engaged in the emerging fields of tissue engineering, drug delivery engineering, bio-inspired computing, and a range of other biotechnological pursuits. As research activities mature, efforts to transition the new knowledge from laboratory products into marketable products will increase and so too will the involvement of engineers. Products will increasingly support commoditized biosystems, ranging from artificial organs and implantable devices to other "sustaining systems." Where technology and life converge, considerations of safety and reliability become paramount. There will be new requirements for engineers to acquire basic knowledge about biological systems and to pay increased attention to areas such as fault-tolerant designs to mitigate liability concerns. The design of biotech products will require knowledge that crosses multiple disciplines (e.g., materials development, computing applications, automated biological processes) in a compelling example of the value of interdisciplinary engineering.

Engineering will also wrestle with problems that today are rooted in biology and chemistry on the microscale. Ongoing concerns about chemical and biological weapons will demand that engineers of all kinds have more than a passing knowledge of these subjects. Future civil engineers (or at least those engineers with the requisite knowledge however designated in 2020) will know about transport characteristics of biological and chemical agents and their diffusivity in air and water supplies. Mechanical engineers will devise pumps and filters that are able to deal with a wide variety of airborne and waterborne chemical or biological agents. Electrical engineers will design sensing and detection instruments capable of providing early warning of the presence of such agents.

Nanotechnology

"Nanoengineering" to create and manufacture structures and materials on a molecular level will continue as a focus for the next few generations of engineers. Nanoscience and nanoengineering draw on multiple fields, as reflected in applications in bioengineering (e.g., genetic and molecular engineering), materials science (composites and engineered materials), and electronics (quantum-scale optical and electrical structures). Nanostructures have been proposed as environmental cleaning agents, chemical detection agents, for the creation of biological (or artificial) organs, for the development of nanoelectronic mechanical systems (NEMS), and for the development of ultrafast, ultradense electrical and optical circuits. In a marriage of engineering and biology to create synthetic biology, efforts are proceeding to create a suite of fundamental tools and techniques to fabricate biological devices, analogous to those used to create microelectronic devices (Ball, 2001; National Research Council, 2003).

The federal government has created the U.S. National Nanotechnology Initiative and in fiscal year 2004 will provide almost $1 billion in research and development funding (see Table 1). The grand challenges identified for this initiative illustrate the breadth of the potential of this new field.

Materials Science and Photonics

Even in traditional areas of engineering, like bridge and automotive design, civil and mechanical engineers will increasingly need to understand new materials that can be used in composites, atomic-scale machines, and molecular-based nanostructures. Smart materials and structures, which have the capability of sensing and responding, for example, to displacements caused by earthquakes and explosions, will be used increasingly. If the present petroleum economy is replaced by a hydrogen economy, fuel cells will replace the internal combustion engine and batteries as power sources, and a general understanding of fuel-cell-

TABLE 1 Challenges Identified for the National Nanotechnology Initiative

Time Frame	Strategic Challenge
Nano-Now	• Pigments in paints
	• Cutting tools and wear resistant coatings
	• Pharmaceuticals and drugs
	• Nanoscale particles and thin films in electronic devices
	• Jewelry, optical, and semiconductor wafer polishing
Nano-2007	• Biosensors, transducers, and detectors
	• Functional designer fluids
	• Propellants, nozzles, and valves
	• Flame retardant additives
	• Drug delivery, biomagnetic separation, and wound healing
Nano-2012	• Nano-optical, nanoelectronics, and nanopower sources
	• High-end flexible displays
	• Nano-bio materials as artificial organs
	• NEMS-based devices
	• Faster switches and ultra-sensitive sensors

SOURCE: Adapted from National Research Council (2002).

powered engines, fuel-cell chemistry, and the materials of fuel cells will be needed. Moreover, as smart materials are used in advanced products, material properties based on mechanical, optical, and electromagnetic interactions become core knowledge topics that support effective engineering practice.

As the physical sizes of optical sources decrease while their power and reliability continue to increase, photonics-based technologies will become more significant in engineered products and systems. Fiber optics communications, precision manufacturing applications (e.g., precision cutting, visioning, sensing), and applications employing free space line-of-sight optical links, laser guidance, and optical sensing and monitoring will continue to advance (Board on Chemical Sciences and Technology, 2003; Suhir, 2000).

Information and Communications Technology

To appreciate the potential of information technology, one has only to consider the remarkable changes that have taken place in U.S. society in the past few decades. Today young adults cannot imagine life without computers, video conferencing, mobile phones, copiers, and the Internet, and most of us who are old enough to have lived without them appreciate them even more. What will happen in the foreseeable future? Today a 1-gigabit hard drive ships in a package $1 \times 1 \times \frac{1}{8}$ inches; soon that will be a 10-gigabit drive, and computers small enough to fit into trouser pockets will be able to contain information that would fill a modern library (Feldman, 2001). The speed and computing power of future desktop machines and software will enable design and simulation capabilities that will make the routine activities of contemporary engineers obsolete, thus freeing them for ever more creative tasks. The world will be networked with broadband communications, allowing huge volumes of information to be transmitted at high data rates for real-time collaboration between engineering design centers anywhere, reshaping our perceptions of connectedness, location, and access. As early as the 1960s, the Advanced Research Project Agency research community began to imagine a world where networks of computer workstations could connect to each other, sharing data, working in parallel on common problems, and advancing computing power to new heights (Brand, 1972; Gates, 1996; Goldberg, 1988). In the developed world, because of the Internet, this is the world we live in today. Everything will, in some sense, be "smart"; that is, every product, every service, and every bit of infrastructure will be attuned to the needs of the humans it serves and will adapt its behavior to those needs.

For engineering the imperative to accommodate connectivity establishes an integral role for core competencies related to electronics, electromagnetics, photonics, and the underlying discrete as well as continuous mathematics. Core competencies in materials and the cultivation of skills related to the use of information technology for communications purposes are also indicated. Engineers and engineering will seek to optimize the benefits derived from a unified appreciation of the physical, psychological, and emotional interactions between information technology and humans. As engineers seek to create products to aid physical and other activities, the strong research base in physiology, ergonomics, and human interactions with computers will expand to include cognition, the processing of information, and physiological responses to electrical, mechanical, and optical stimulation.

Given the expected role of computers in the future, it is essential that engineers of all disciplines have a deep working knowledge of the fundamentals of digital systems as well as fluency in using contemporary computer systems and tools. Many, if not all, engineering systems in the future will be digital systems. Advances in computing and simulation, coupled with technologies that mimic rudimentary attributes in analysis, may radically redefine common practices in engineering. There will be growth in areas of simulation and modeling around the creation of new engineering "structures." Computer-based design-build engineering, such as was done with the Boeing 777 and is commonly done in civil engineering, will become the norm for most product designs, accelerating the creation of complex structures for which multiple subsystems combine to form a final product.

The Information Explosion

Surrounding all these technologies is the growth of data and knowledge at an exponential rate. A few hundred years ago it was conceivable for a person to be conversant about much of the science, mathematics, medicine, music, and art of the day. Today, in an age of specialization, an individual's area of expertise continues to diminish in relation to the total body of technical knowledge. The health care field offers a daunting example of the future; there will be more new knowledge created in the next few years than in all previous history. Beginning in the early 1990s, data management requirements in life sciences-based engineering activities began to outpace Moore's law (see Figure 1). These data will drive and be driven by the biotechnology revolution. Memory access rates and manipulation of databases will represent an ongoing challenge to efficiently and effectively mine these data.

In the past, engineering responded to the explosion in knowledge by continually developing and spawning new areas of focus in the various engineering disciplines. As more of these areas arise, the depth of individual knowledge increases, but the breadth can dramatically decrease. This poses a challenge to an engineering future where interdisciplinarity will likely be critical to the solution of complex problems.

Logistics

The combination of wireless connectivity, handheld computers, and inventory tracking and database software has modernized logistics.

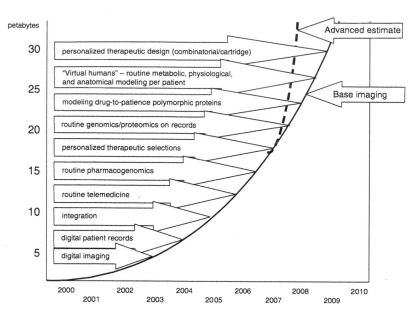

FIGURE 1 Life sciences data management requirements. Advanced Imaging: Optimistic projections assuming 5×10^7 accessible population with each person requiring 82×10^9 bytes by 2010–2012. This is primarily based on an assumption that advanced 3D/4D imaging capabilities hold ~80% of medical storage. Base Estimate: Assumes clinical and biomedical use will be at least 30% of 2010 total world storage, conservatively set at 100 petabytes. Downplays advanced imaging capabilities.
SOURCE: Copyright International Business Machines Corporation, 2004.

Companies in the transportation sector were the first to embrace logistics as a tool to help organize activities while improving productivity. Manufacturing and retail companies as diverse as Ford, Boeing, Intel, and Wal-Mart are heavily dependent on logistics to link together their far-flung networks of suppliers and manufacturing units. Especially in the past decade, outsourcing and "just-in-time" manufacturing have turned logistics into a tightly balanced ballet that allows companies to work across continents to develop products and deliver them at the right time and place around the world. Market success or failure hangs in the balance.

Logistics is being taught in an increasing number of engineering curricula and is steadily becoming a more sophisticated field. It has led to the creation of new jobs for engineers in industries and companies that traditionally did not employ them. The challenge of moving goods and services more efficiently will likely engage engineering up to and through 2020.

TECHNOLOGICAL CHALLENGES

The engineer of 2020 will need to be conversant with and embrace a whole realm of new technologies, but some old problems are not going to go away. They will demand new attention and, perhaps, new technologies. In some cases their continuing neglect will move them from problems to crises.

Physical Infrastructures in Urban Settings

Previous approaches to urban development reflected attention to human services and private-sector requirements without a sufficient focus on environmental impact and sustainability. The result is that many large cities today are victims of pollution, traffic and transportation infrastructure concerns, decreasing greenery, poor biodiversity, and disparate educational services. In general, though, the United States has arguably had the best physical infrastructure in the developed world. The concern is that these infrastructures are in serious decline, and hence aging water treatment, waste disposal, transportation, and energy facilities are among the top concerns for public officials and citizens alike. In 2003 the American Society of Civil Engineers (ASCE) issued an update to its 2001 report card on America's aging infrastructure. Each category in the ASCE reports was evaluated on the basis of condition and performance, capacity versus need, and funding versus need. The assessments do not include security enhancements as no authoritative data on these upgrades are available. The 2003 report gives America an overall grade of D+ on its physical infrastructure and estimates that $1.6 trillion would be needed to restore it over the five-year period beginning in 2004 (see Table 2).

The 2001 report card (see Table 3) provides additional detail. The longer these investments are pushed into the future, the more likely the state of deteriorating infrastructures will reach crisis proportions. Engi-

TABLE 2 America's Aging Infrastructure, 2003

Area	Grade	Trend (since 2001)
Roads	D+	↓
Bridges	C	↔
Transit	C−	↓
Aviation	D	↔
Schools	D−	↔
Drinking Water	D	↓
Wastewater	D	↓
Dams	D	↓
Solid waste	C+	↔
Hazardous waste	D+	↔
Navigable waterways	D+	↓
Energy	D+	↓
America's Infrastructure GPA	D+	
• Total Investment		$1.6 Trillion (estimated five-year need)

SOURCE: Adapted from American Society of Civil Engineers (2003).

neering is ideally positioned to help address these issues given the will of public leaders and the general public to make the required investments. The arrows in the rightmost column of Table 2 indicate how the state of the infrastructure has changed since the 2001 report; horizontal arrows indicate no change, and an arrow pointing down indicates further degradation.

Information and Communications Infrastructure

Because it is of more recent vintage, the nation's information and telecommunications infrastructure has not suffered nearly as much degradation due to the ravages of time, but vulnerabilities due to accidental or intentional events are well recognized and are a serious concern. Recent evidence has shown that malicious attacks (such as computer viruses and denial of service attacks), system overloads (as in the case of the disruptions in wireless phone service in the aftermath of the September 11 attacks), and natural disasters (such as hurricanes and earthquakes, which disrupt the electricity grid that underlies the information and communications infrastructure), can have a profound

TABLE 3 America's Aging Infrastructure, 2001

Area	Grade	Note
Roads	D+	One-third of the nation's major roads are in poor or mediocre condition, costing American drivers an estimated $5.8 billion per year.
Bridges	C	As of 1998, 29 percent of the nation's bridges were structurally deficient or functionally obsolete, an improvement from 31 percent in 1996.
Transit	C–	Transit ridership has increased 15 percent since 1995. Capital spending must increase 41 percent just to maintain the system in its present condition.
Aviation	D	Airport capacity has increased only 1 percent in the past 10 years, while air traffic increased 37 percent during that time. Congestion also jeopardizes safety—there were 429 runway incursions ("near misses") reported in 2000, up 25 percent from 1999.
Schools	D–	Due to either aging/outdated facilities or severe overcrowding, 75 percent of our nation's school buildings are inadequate to meet the needs of schoolchildren. The average cost of capital investment needed is $3,800 per student, more than half the average cost to educate a student for one year. Since 1998 the total need has increased from $112 billion to $127 billion.
Drinking Water	D	The nation's 54,000 drinking water systems face an annual shortfall of $11 billion needed to replace facilities that are nearing the end of their useful life and to comply with federal water regulations.
Wastewater	D	The nation's 16,000 wastewater systems face enormous needs. Some sewer systems are 100 years old. Currently, there is a $12 billion annual shortfall in funding for infrastructure needs in this category.
Energy	D+	Since 1990, actual capacity has increased only about 7,000 megawatts (MW) per year, an annual shortfall of 30 percent. More than 10,000 MW of capacity will have to be added each year until 2008 to keep up with the 1.8 percent annual growth in demand.
Hazardous Waste	D+	Effective regulation and enforcement have largely halted the contamination of new sites. Aided by the best cleanup technology in the world, the rate of Superfund cleanup has quickened—though not enough to keep pace with the number of new sites listed as the backlog of potential sites is assessed.

SOURCE: Adapted from American Society of Civil Engineers (2003).

impact on our national economy, our national security, our lifestyles, and our sense of personal security, if not our actual personal security (Computer Science Telecommunications Board, 2003). It falls to both the public and the private sectors to develop strategies and take actions to continually update the infrastructure to keep pace with technological advances, to increase capacity to respond to the rapid growth in information and communications technology-related services, to develop and design systems with a global perspective, to work to increase security and reliability, and to consider issues of privacy (Crishna et al., 2000). These actions will clearly involve legal, regulatory, economic, business, and social considerations, but engineering innovation is and will remain a critical factor in the effort to operate, expand, devise upgrades to, and reduce the vulnerabilities of these systems.

The Environment

A number of natural resource and environmental concerns will frame our world's challenges for the 21st century. For example, in 2020 the state of California will need the equivalent of 40 percent more electrical capacity, 40 percent more gasoline, and 20 percent more natural gas energy than was needed in the year 2000 (California Business, Transportation, and Housing Agency, 2001). Global per capita forest area is projected to fall to one-third of its 1990 value by 2020 (Forest and Agriculture Organization of the United Nations, 1995), and most of this reduction will be due to population growth in tropical areas and shrinking forest area. Forty-eight countries containing a total of 2.8 billion people could face freshwater shortages by 2025 (Hinrichsen et al., 1997).

The question of water is at the heart of a 600-page world water development report recently issued by the United Nations (2003). The report projects that within the next 20 years virtually every nation in the world will face some type of water supply problem. Water tables are falling in China, India, and the United States, which together produce half the world's food. Presently it is estimated that more than a billion people have little access to clean drinking water and that 2 billion live in conditions of water scarcity. In their article *Who Owns Water*, Barlow and Clarke (2002) write: "Quite simply, unless we dramatically change our ways, between one-half and two-thirds of humanity will be living with severe fresh water shortages within the next quarter century." Water supplies will affect the future of the world's economy and its stability.

If we are to preserve our environment for future generations (see Chapter 2) we must develop and implement more ecologically sustainable practices as we seek to achieve economic prosperity. Sustainable practices must proceed apace in industrialized countries and developing countries alike. If sustainability is pursued only in industrialized countries, where the resources are available, they will remain islands in a sea of environmentally bereft developing countries. It is becoming increasingly apparent, though, that design criteria and standards suitable for industrialized countries must be adjusted for the local conditions in developed countries if sustainability projects hope to succeed. The engineer of 2020 will have to understand how to adapt solutions, in an ethical way, to the constraints of developing countries.

The fossil fuel supply, global warming, depletion of the ozone layer, misdistribution of water use, and the loss of forests have been described by some as "extinction-level" crises (Hinrichsen and Robey, 2000). It is difficult to know how the flow of resources will vary over the next several decades, but it is certain that, along with conservation, technological innovation must be part of the solution to circumvent, or at least mitigate, these crises. Engineering practices must incorporate attention to sustainable technology, and engineers need to be educated to consider issues of sustainability in all aspects of design and manufacturing.

As codified at a recent conference on sustainability, green engineering is the design, commercialization, and use of processes and products that are feasible and economical while minimizing the generation of pollution at the source and the risk to human health and the environment (National Science Foundation, 2003). The discipline embraces the concept that decisions to protect human health and the environment can have the greatest impact and cost effectiveness when applied early to the design and development phase of a process or product.

Table 4 presents the nine guiding principles developed at the *Green Engineering: Defining Principles Conference* (National Science Foundation, 2003). The principles point to systems-based strategies and holistic approaches that embed social and cultural objectives into the traditional engineering focus on technical and economic viability.

TABLE 4 Guiding Principles in Green Engineering

Engineer processes and products holistically, use systems analysis, and integrate environmental impact assessment tools.

Conserve and improve natural ecosystems while protecting human health and well-being.

Use life-cycle thinking in all engineering activities.

Ensure that all material and energy inputs and outputs are as inherently safe and benign as possible.

Minimize depletion of natural resources.

Strive to prevent waste.

Develop and apply engineering solutions while being cognizant of local geography, aspirations, and cultures.

Create engineering solutions beyond current or dominant technologies; improve, innovate, and invent (technologies) to achieve sustainability.

Actively engage communities and stakeholders in the development of engineering solutions.

SOURCE: Adapted from National Science Foundation (2003).

Technology for an Aging Population

Engineering can be an agent for addressing the challenges of aging. New technologies are on the horizon that can help aging citizens maintain healthy, productive lifestyles well beyond conventional retirement age. One emerging area of study, assistive technology, has a central focus on creating technologies that accommodate people of all ages who are challenged by physical and other limitations. In an aging society, opportunities will grow in the area of assistive technology.

The Center for Aging Services Technologies (2003) has identified several areas where future investment would significantly improve services to aging patients. These include technologies, such as monitors, sensors, robots, and smart housing, that would allow elder persons to maintain independent lifestyles and alleviate the burdens placed on care providers and government programs; operational technologies that would help service providers reduce labor costs or prevent medical errors; connective technologies that would help elderly patients communicate with caregivers, families, and medical resources; and telemedicine to provide basic or specialized services to patients in remote locations or to amplify their access to a broad range of medical services.

Assistive technology
includes technologies in education, rehabilitation, and independent living to help, to change, or to train physically challenged citizens. People of all ages with physical, cognitive, and communication disorders, or a combination of disabilities, may benefit from the application of assistive technologies.
www.katsnet.org

IMPLICATIONS FOR ENGINEERING EDUCATION

The Technology Explosion

Since the late 19th century, when the major subdisciplines of engineering began to emerge, engineers have been aware that solutions to many societal problems lie at the interstices of subdisciplines. In 1960 the Advanced Research Projects Agency of the U.S. Department of Defense established Materials Research Centers (MRCs); later the National Science Foundation assumed operation of the MRC program and created Engineering Research Centers, both in recognition of the value of providing an environment where engineers and scientists of different backgrounds could join together to solve interdisciplinary problems. As valuable as such centers are, students are still largely assigned to and educated in a single department, and, as engineering disciplines have proliferated and clearly delineated specialties within those subdisciplines have evolved, providing a broad engineering education to students has become an enormous challenge. This challenge will only become more daunting as the information on new science and technology continues to explode and new and totally unanticipated technologies, requiring even more specialization, emerge in the future. Engineering education must avoid the cliché of teaching more and more about less and less, until it teaches everything about nothing. Addressing this problem may involve reconsideration of the basic structure of engineering departments and the infrastructure for evaluating the performance of professors as much as it does selecting the coursework students should be taught.

The Pace of Change

Scientific and engineering knowledge doubles every 10 years (Wright, 1999). This geometric growth rate has been reflected in an accelerating rate of technology introduction and adoption. Product cycles continue to decrease, and each cycle delivers more functional and often less expensive versions of existing products, occasionally introduces entirely new "disruptive" technologies, and makes older technologies obsolete at an increasing rate. The comfortable notion that a person learns all that he or she needs to know in a four-year engineering program just is not true and never was. Not even the "fundamentals" are fixed, as new technologies enter the engineer's toolkit. Engineers are going to have to accept responsibility for their own continual re-education, and engineering schools are going to have to prepare engineers to do so by teaching them how to learn. Engineering schools should also consider organizational structures that will allow continuous programmatic adaptation to satisfy the professional needs of the engineering workforce that are changing at an increasing rate. Meeting the demands of the rapidly changing workforce calls for reconsideration of standards for faculty qualifications, appointments, and expectations.

CONCLUSION

The engineer of 2020 will be faced with myriad challenges, creating offensive and defensive solutions at the macro- and microscales in preparation for possible dramatic changes in the world. Engineers will be expected to anticipate and prepare for potential catastrophes such as biological terrorism; water and food contamination; infrastructure damage to roads, bridges, buildings, and the electricity grid; and communications breakdown in the Internet, telephony, radio, and television. Engineers will be asked to create solutions that minimize the risk of complete failure and at the same time prepare backup solutions that enable rapid recovery, reconstruction, and deployment. In short, they will face problems qualitatively similar to those they already face today.

To solve the new problems, however, they can be expected to create an array of new and possibly revolutionary tools and technologies. These will embody the core knowledge and skills that will support effective engineering education and a sense of engineering professionalism in the new century. The challenge for the profession and engineering education is to ensure that the core knowledge advances in information technology, nanoscience, biotechnology, materials science, photonics (Smerdon, 2002), and other areas yet to be discovered are delivered to engineering students so they can leverage them to achieve inter-disciplinary solutions to engineering problems in their engineering practice. The rapidly changing nature of modern knowledge and technology will demand, even more so than today, that engineers so educated must embrace continuing education as a career development strategy with the same fervor that continuous improvement has been embraced by the manufacturing community.

REFERENCES

American Society of Civil Engineers. 2003. Report Card on America's Aging Infrastructure. Washington, D.C.: ASCE.

Awschalom, D.D., M.E. Flatté, and N. Samarth. 2002. Microelectronic devices that function by using the spin of the electron are a nascent multibillion-dollar industry—and may lead to quantum microchips. Available online at: *http://www.ScientificAmerica.com.*

Ball, P. 2001. Biology Goes Back to the Drawing Board. Nature, February 12.

Barlow, M., and T. Clarke. 2002. Who Owns Water? The Nation, September 2. Available online at: *http://www.thenation.com/doc.mhtml?i=20020902&s=barlow.*

Board on Chemical Sciences and Technology. 2003. Materials Science and Technology: Challenges for the Chemical Sciences in the 21st Century. Washington, D.C.: The National Academies Press.

Brand, S. 1972. Spacewar: Fanatic Life and Symbolic Death Among the Computer Bums. Rolling Stone Magazine, December 7. Available online at: *http://www.wheels.org/spacewar/stone/rolling_stone.html.*

California Business, Transportation, and Housing Agency. 2001. Invest for California: Strategic Planning for California's Future Prosperity and Quality of Life. Report of the California Business, Transportation, and Housing Agency Commission on Building for the 21st Century, Sacramento, Calif. Available online at: *http://www.bth.ca.gov/invest4cal/.*

Center for Aging Services Technologies. 2003. Progress and Possibilities: State of Technology and Aging Services. Publication of the American Association of Homes and Services for the Aging, Washington, D.C. Available online at *http://www.agingtech.org.*

Crishna, V., N. Baqai, B.R. Pandey, and F. Rahman. 2000. Telecommunications Infrastructure: A Long Way to Go. Publication of the South Asia Networks Organisation, Dhaka, Bangladesh. Available online at: *http://www.sasianet.org.*

Computer Science Telecommunications Board. 2003. The Internet Under Crisis Conditions: Learning from September 11. Washington, D.C.: The National Academies Press.

Feldman, S. 2001. Presentation at Impact of Information Technology on the Future of the Research University Workshop, panel on Technology Futures, National Research Council, Washington, D.C., January 22-23.

Forest and Agriculture Organization of the United Nations. 1995. Forest Resources Assessment 1990: Tropical Forest Plantation Resources. FAO Forestry Paper 128. Rome, Italy.

Gates, W. 1996. The Road Ahead. Highbridge, N.J.: Penguin Group.

Goldberg, A., ed. 1988. A History of Personal Workstations. New York: Addison-Wesley Publishing.

Hinrichsen, D., and B. Robey. 2000. Population and the Environment: The Global Challenge. Baltimore, Md.: Population Information Program, Johns Hopkins School of Public Health.

Hinrichsen, D., B. Robey, and U.D. Upadhyay. 1997. Solutions for a Water-Short World. Baltimore, Md.: Population Information Program, Johns Hopkins School of Public Health.

Kuhn, T. 1970 (1962). The Structure of Scientific Revolutions, 2nd Edition. Chicago: University of Chicago Press.

Mittelstrass, J. 2001. How to Maintain the Technical Momentum and Ability in the Knowledge Economy. Keynote presentation at Linking Knowledge and Society: A European Council of Applied Sciences and Engineering Conference, Royal Academy Palace, Brussels, Belgium, October 16.

National Research Council. 2001. Workshop on Bio-inspired Computing. Committee on the Frontiers Between the Interface of Computing and Biology. Irvine, Calif. January 31.

National Research Council. 2002. Small Wonders, Endless Frontiers: A Review of the National Nanotechnology Initiative. Washington, D.C.: The National Academies Press.

National Research Council. 2003. Hierarchical Structure in Biology as a Guide for New Materials Technology. Washington, D.C.: The National Academies Press.

National Science Foundation. 2003. Conference report on Green Engineering: Defining Principles, San Destin, Fl. May 18-22, Available online at: *http://enviro.utoledo.edu/Green/SanDestin%20summary.pdf.*

Smerdon, E. 2002. Presentation at The Engineer of 2020 Visioning and Scenario-Development Workshop, Woods Hole, Mass. September 3-4.

Suhir, E. 2000. The Future of Microelectronics and Photonics and the Role of Mechanical, Materials, and Reliability Engineering. Keynote presentation at MicroMaterials Conference 2000, Berlin. April 17-19. Speech outline available online at: *http://www.ieee.org/organizations/tab/newtech/workshops/ntdc_2001_18.pdf.*

United Nations. 2003. Water for People, Water for Life—UN World Water Development Report. New York: UNESCO.

Wright, B.T. 1999. Knowledge Management. Presentation at meeting of Industry-University-Government Roundtable on Enhancing Engineering Education, Iowa State University, Ames. May 24.

2

Societal, Global, and Professional Contexts of Engineering Practice

SOCIAL CONTEXT

The future is uncertain. However, one thing is clear: engineering will not operate in a vacuum separate from society in 2020 any more than it does now. Both on a macro scale, where the world's natural resources will be stressed by population increases, to the micro scale, where engineers need to work in teams to be effective, consideration of social issues is central to engineering. Political and economic relations between nations and their peoples will impact engineering practice in the future, probably to a greater extent than now. Attention to intellectual property, project management, multilingual influences and cultural diversity, moral/religious repercussions, global/international impacts, national security, and cost-benefit constraints will continue to drive engineering practice.

Population and Demographics

By the year 2020 the world's population will approach 8 billion people, and much of that increase will be among groups that today are outside the developed nations[1] (Central Intelligence Agency, 2001). Of

---

[1]Developed nations as defined by the World Bank are countries with a gross national product equal to or greater than $10,000 per person.

the 1.5 billion people that the world's population will gain by 2020, most will be added to countries in Asia and Africa (see Figure 2). By 2015, and for the first time in history, the majority of people, mostly poor (see Figure 3), will reside in urban centers, mostly in countries that lack the economic, social, and physical infrastructures to support a burgeoning population. By 2050, if work retirement patterns remain the same, the ratio of taxpaying workers to nonworking pensioners in the developed world will fall from 4:1 to 2:1. Hence, in 2020 the world will be more crowded and will have more centers of dense population, and the potential is high that many people will live in regions with fewer technological resources. These factors present several challenges for society and multiple opportunities for the application of thought-fully constructed solutions through the work of engineers.

A review of the 2000 U.S. census indicates a proportional increase in minority populations. During the 1990s, the combined populations of African Americans, Native Americans, Asians, Pacific Islanders, and Hispanics/Latinos grew at 13 times the rate of the non-Hispanic white population. Table 5 summarizes the demographic statistics by age, gender, and race/ethnicity. Most notable is the increase in the number of Hispanic Americans, which now surpasses the African American population. The U.S. Hispanic population grew 58 percent between 1990 and 2000.

If current trends continue, Hispanic Americans will account for 17 percent of the U.S. population by 2020, and African Americans 12.8 percent. The percentage of whites will decline from the 2000 value of 75.6 percent to 63.7 percent. Looking further into the future, by 2050, almost half of the U.S. population will be non-white (U.S. Census Bureau, 2002). Thus, in 2020 and beyond, the engineering profession will need to develop solutions that are acceptable to an increasingly diverse population and will need to draw more students from sectors that traditionally have not been well represented in the engineering workforce.

Health and Health Care

We cannot think about population growth and distribution in 2020 without considering human health and health care delivery. Citizens of 2020, as now, will look to their leaders to close the health care gaps related to technology and access. Through the development of innova-

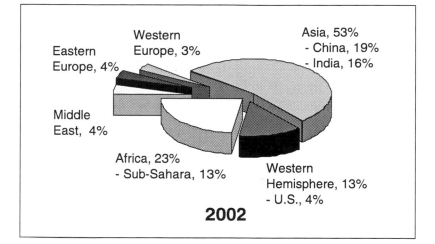

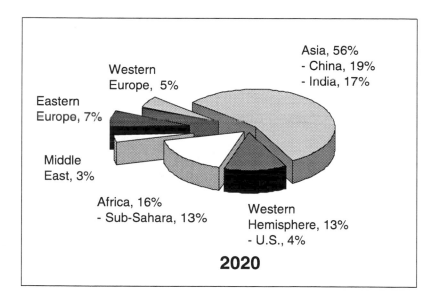

FIGURE 2 Distribution of world population in a mix of 100 people in 2002 (upper) and 2020 (lower). SOURCE: Adapted from Central Intelligence Agency (2001).

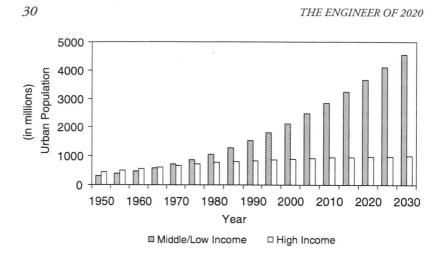

FIGURE 3 Urban population growth. SOURCE: Adapted from United Nations (2002).

tive strategies that support highly individualized volume production, cost effectiveness, and sustainability, new engineering technologies may provide an ideal avenue to make advanced medical technologies accessible to a global population base. In the developed world, it is plausible to believe that in 20 years pollution and air quality in urban environments will be much improved, as will cleanup and control of hazardous waste sites, and debilitating diseases, old and new, driven by such environmental factors will have a much reduced impact on human health. Health care delivery in developing countries will continue to lag that in the developed world, but well-focused efforts to control AIDS and malaria may meet with increasing success.

Thus, along with population growth, the demographics of the world's population will change. As new knowledge on health and health care is created, shifts in life expectancies will lead to an increase in the number of people living well beyond established retirement ages. In 2004, 20 percent of the people residing in Italy will be over age 65; by 2020, China, Australia, Russia, Canada, and the United States will face a similar situation (Central Intelligence Agency, 2001). The impacts of an aging society are multiple. First is the economic stress. In an aging society, health and health care and quality of life are critical areas of focus. Currently, citizens generally participate in the workforce until

TABLE 5 Resident Population of the United States by Age, Gender, and Race/Ethnicity

	1990		2000		2020	
	Number	Percent	Number	Percent	Number	Percent
Total Population	248,709,873	100.0	281,421,906	100.0	324,926,000	100.0
Under age 18	63,604,432	25.6	72,293,812	25.7	77,151,000	23.7
Ages 18 to 64	153,863,610	61.9	174,136,341	61.9	194,043,000	59.7
Ages 65 and over	31,241,831	12.6	34,991,753	12.4	53,733,922	16.5
Males	121,239,418	48.7	138,053,563	49.1	158,856,000	48.9
Females	127,470,455	51.3	143,368,343	50.9	166,071,000	51.1
Whites	188,128,296	75.6	194,552,774	69.1	207,145,000	63.7
Blacks	29,216,293	11.7	33,947,837	12.1	41,548,000	12.8
Hispanics	22,354,059	9.0	35,305,818	12.5	55,156,000	17.0
Asians	6,968,359	2.8	10,476,678	3.7	18,527,000	5.7
American Indians	1,793,773	0.7	2,068,883	0.7	2,549,000	0.8

SOURCE: Adapted from U.S. Census Bureau (2002)

they reach the age of 65. With increases in life expectancy, fewer young workers are available to help pay for the services older citizens expect, and stresses on economic systems will occur. According to the Congressional Budget Office, Social Security, Medicare, and Medicaid currently account for 7.5 percent of the U.S. gross domestic product, but this figure may reach 16.4 percent in 2040 (Lee and Haaga, 2002).[2] Additionally, the aging population makes greater demands on the health care system, heightens labor force tensions, and increases political instability (Central Intelligence Agency, 2001). The engineering profession of 2020 will have to operate in this environment, which may include "senior" engineers who are willing, able, and perhaps compelled to work by economic necessity.

The Youth Bulge and Security Implications

In contrast to the aging trend, nations in many politically unstable parts of the world will experience a "youth bulge," a disproportionate number of 15- to 29-year-olds in the general population; globally, more than 50 percent of the world's population could be less than 18 years old in 2020. The youth bulge is expected to be most prominent in Sub-Saharan Africa, Afghanistan, Pakistan, Mexico, and countries of the Middle East—all developing nations. Countries that have in the recent past experienced youth bulge conditions include Iran, Northern Ireland, Gaza, and Sri Lanka—all regions of recent social and political tensions exacerbated by an excess of idle youths unable to find employment. As a consequence, the world could face continuing social and political unrest and threats from terrorism and fundamentalism, creating an increased need for military services and security measures at home and abroad. Many hold out the hope that migration from the youth bulge countries to the rapidly aging countries will mitigate the projected problems related to aging and the youth bulge. In the face of heightened concerns about terrorism, however, the United States would probably permit this immigration only as a very carefully metered trickle. This could seriously depress the supply of foreign engineers and increase the need for engineering schools to recruit, nurture, and retain domestic students.

---

[2]It must be noted that the long-range estimate is highly sensitive to health costs, actual population trends, and actual economic productivity.

The Accelerating Global Economy

The world's economy has become tightly linked, with much of the change triggered by technology itself. Three hundred years ago the advent of ships with navigation tools and reliable clocks allowed nations to engage in commerce that was previously unthinkable. Later, communication technologies like the telegraph opened new horizons to multinational trade. Yet it has been the latest evolution, keyed by the maturation of the Internet and a global advanced telecommunications network of satellites and optical fibers, that is creating a new order, where services and information can be provided on one side of the globe and delivered instantly to meet demands on the other side. The dramatic possibilities offered by this development are being fueled by rapidly improving educational capabilities in countries like China and India and the availability of highly skilled workers with engineering and science backgrounds in these and other countries, willing and able to work for wages well below those in the developed nations. It is estimated that today China is producing more than twice the graduates in mechanical engineering and more than three times the graduates in all fields of engineering than is the United States (Ehler, 2003).

In this new global economy, high-end services like electronic design, applied research, accounting, aerospace design, technical consulting, and x-ray assessment can be done more economically outside the developed world and the results transmitted electronically back to the developed countries. Thus, new semiconductors can be readily designed in China and India and used to manufacture chips anywhere in the world.

Many advanced engineering designs are accomplished using virtual global teams—highly integrated engineering teams comprised of researchers located around the world. These teams often function across multiple time zones, multiple cultures, and sometimes multiple languages. They also can operate asynchronously. Analogously, Internet-based enterprises allow businesses to grow based on a virtual customer base for advertising and commerce that expands the globe. The customer can shop anytime and anywhere. Hence, information sharing has the effect of tying cultures, knowledge, and economies, with both possible positive and negative impacts on U.S.-based engineers. These impacts will become more ubiquitous as Internet connectivity expands in underdeveloped areas of the globe (see Figure 4).

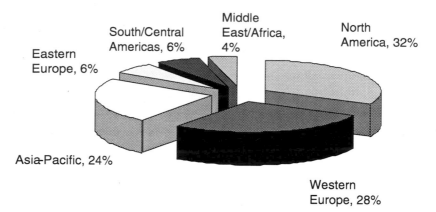

FIGURE 4 Demographics for Internet usage in 2005. SOURCE: Adapted from Central Intelligence Agency (2001).

PROFESSIONAL CONTEXT FOR ENGINEERS IN THE FUTURE

The Systems Perspective

In the past, steady increases in knowledge have spawned new microdisciplines within engineering (e.g., microelectronics, photonics, biomechanics). However, contemporary challenges—from biomedical devices to complex manufacturing designs to large systems of networked devices—increasingly require a *systems* perspective. Systems engineering is based on the principle that structured methodologies can be used to integrate components and technologies. The systems perspective is one that looks to achieve synergy and harmony among diverse components of a larger theme. Hence, there is a need for greater breadth so that broader requirements can be addressed. Many believe this necessitates new ways of *doing* engineering.

Working in Teams

Because of the increasing complexity and scale of systems-based engineering problems, there is a growing need to pursue collaborations with multidisciplinary teams of experts across multiple fields. Essential attributes for these teams include excellence in communication (with technical and public audiences), an ability to communicate using technology, and an understanding of the complexities associated with a global market and social context. Flexibility, receptiveness to change, and mutual respect are essential as well. For example, it already is found that engineers may come together in teams based on individual areas of expertise and disperse once a challenge has been addressed, only to regroup again differently to respond to a new challenge.

Only recently have strategies for ensuring effectiveness in interdisciplinary engineering teams been discussed among engineering educators (Fruchter, 2002; Smith, 2003). Much of our existing knowledge about teams and how they can best be assembled and managed has been developed through other disciplines (e.g., business, psychology, other social sciences). However, a number of researchers have recognized a need to tailor and adapt this existing knowledge to support engineering teams and organizations (Bordogna, 1997; Shuman et al., 2002; Smerdon, 2003). For engineering this topic, including the challenge of working effectively with multicultural teams, will continue to grow in importance as systems engineering becomes more pervasive.

Complexity

Engineers must know how and when to incorporate social elements into a comprehensive systems analysis of their work. This changing landscape for engineering can be illustrated in a complexity model developed by the committee that indicates that it is not just the nature of a narrow technical challenge but the legal, market, political, etc., landscape and constraints that will characterize the way the challenge is addressed. The model helps categorize how and why engineers approach problems and illustrates the types of challenges engineering will address. A two-dimensional matrix considering "old versus new" methodologies used to tackle "old versus new" challenges defines four different approaches (see Figure 5). The matrix also illustrates the way these problem-solving approaches are influenced by cost sensitivity and confidence in the solution.

Cost Sensitivity

←————————————

	New Ways/Old Problems	New Ways/New Problems
New Ways	• Design for recycling • Retrofits/redesigns • Pulls from a diverse set of tools & experience • More application reuse • Required regression suites • Cost-benefit analysis • Justification/litigation exposure • National defense (terrorism, etc.) • Existing standards do not support desired application • Maximum exposure since solution has to overcome perceived/real expectations. Tolerance for failure low • Driven by "it has to be better"	• Simulation/modeling complex systems • Liability surrounding the digital work-place • Collaboration—this is where the amount/scale of required information is so deep • Have to consider/scan prior art but look at it in a "new light" • Radically innovative applications of new technology, new literature, or no established/formal standards • Keen eye on differentiation and intellectual capital protection (patent or trade secret) • Prerequisite technologies do not exist (measurement, etc.) • Driven by "desire to conquer/necessity"
Old Ways	• Tacit knowledge retention issues • Host of accepted standards and background information • Aging systems/support requirements • Maintenance of existing infrastructure (including nuclear industry, weapons, computer systems, aging support staff) • Driven by "If it ain't broke . . ."	• Formal, in-depth analysis • Broader application of processes • Functional team-based • Object reuse • Standard development process (research → requirements → design → development → test) • Particularly challenging due to breadth of knowledge space • Driven by "Been there, done that"
	Old Ways/Old Problems	Old Ways/New Problems

Solution Confidence →

FIGURE 5 Complexity model.

Customerization

The explosion in knowledge sharing, coupled with advances in technology, will provide the ability to achieve a new era in *customerization*—a buyer-centric business strategy that combines mass customization with customized marketing (Wind and Rangaswamy, 2000). This will demand the social interaction of engineers with customers, even more so than today, belying the image of the engineer as the techie nerd and demanding that engineers have well-developed people skills. The situation will be the antithesis of the time in 1914 when Henry Ford stated that "every American could have a Ford in any color, so long as it is black." The limitations that once constrained our ability to achieve controlled variability in a mass production environment will no longer exist.

New tools in manufacturing and production, new knowledge about the products being produced and the customers that use them, and the ease with which information and products can be transferred will enable the creation of products and services that are uniquely designed for the user. Manufacturers will have the ability to embed adaptive features into automated processes, including the capacity to respond to real-time information provided by the user and/or other entities. Consumers will demand products that are tailored to their needs and intended uses based on the most unique attributes (e.g., DNA type, physical attributes, specific use environment, or customer preference). The concept of made-to-order products will continue to expand (Tersine and Harvey, 1998), and for many industries a made-to-order ability may become a necessity for survival in the near term. Engineers will be asked to accelerate and expand customerization as businesses compete to build and maintain a strong customer base, wherever those customers may be.

If this is the world that emerges, present concerns about outsourcing of low-wage, mass-production manufacturing jobs may be misplaced. Instead, the concern should be about creating a workforce and business environment that prospers in a mass-production-less economy. Engineers will be central to such a workforce, but what will they need to know and do?

Public Policy

In many ways the roles that engineers take on have always extended beyond the realm of knowledge and technology. In fact, engineering impacts the health and vitality of a nation as no other profession does. The business competitiveness, military strength, health, and standard of living of a nation are intimately connected to engineering. And as technology becomes increasingly engrained into every facet of our lives, the convergence between engineering and public policy will also increase. This new level of intimacy necessitates that engineering (and engineers) develop a stronger sense of how technology and public policy interact.

For example, engineers will need to understand the policy by-products of new technologies, and public servants will need to recognize the engineering implications of policy decisions. Whether the issues involve the environment, energy, health care, education, or national defense, engineering will be integral to developing and maintaining the desired infrastructure in support of policy decisions. Similarly, the introduction of new technologies and products will change the landscape in which those infrastructures exist.

Today, engineers indirectly pursue connections to public policy through lobbying organizations and their own professional societies and think tanks. These groups typically seek to inform and influence legislation. Engineers also participate in community-based organizations—for example nongovernmental organizations that help support the development of underdeveloped and economically disadvantaged communities and nations. However, engagement of engineers in public policy issues has been haphazard at best. It is both the responsibility of engineers and important to the image of the profession that engineers make a better connection in the future.

Public Understanding of Engineering

The American public is generally quite eager to adopt new technology but, ironically, is woefully technology illiterate and unprepared to participate in discussions of the potential dangers of new technologies or discussions of the value of the national investment in research and development. As new technologies continue to emerge at a breakneck pace, this situation can only worsen, absent intervention. As educational institutions, engineering schools should reach out to the semicaptive audience they have of nonengineering majors by offering an exciting course (or courses) that introduces technological concepts of real-world value. Encouraging greater understanding of the value of engineering and the contributions it makes to society can help attract undecided students to engineering as well.

Building on Past Successes and Failures

As we contemplate the engineer of 2020, it is important to capture lessons learned from the rich history of engineering innovation in society. Loren Graham documents a series of engineering failures in the

Soviet Union based on a recurring tendency to neglect labor issues and repeated inattention to the importance of a process to achieve desired safety objectives (Graham, 1993). Recent events associated with the U.S. space program and the power grid have also highlighted the importance of safety protocols and the need to consistently implement those protocols. It is often seen that errors made today are not much different from those that led to failures in times past. Our vulnerability to repeat the mistakes of the past can be reduced, and our opportunities to emulate elegant successes can be improved, through a strategy of reviewing case studies.

IMPLICATIONS FOR ENGINEERING EDUCATION

An Aging Population

The engineer of 2020 will operate in a world with a larger fraction of older citizens, but they will enjoy better health, will remain capable of productive work, and may be compelled to work to decrease the economic demands on the social safety net. The engineering workforce will be swelled by those working past age 65, and this shift in demographics may seriously depress new job opportunities and therefore decrease enrollment at many engineering schools to subcritical levels. Professorial staff cutbacks could exacerbate the difficulty of delivering the breadth of technology demanded for a well-educated engineer in 2020. To retain staff members and keep them fully engaged, engineering schools may have to create new engineering degree programs to attract a new pool of students interested in a less rigorous engineering program as a "liberal" education. While this will not produce more ready-to-practice engineers (who, in this scenario, would face a bleak job market anyway), it will produce more technologically literate students who hopefully will understand the principles of the inquiry-based scientific method and engineering under constraint and be able to apply them to the profession they choose to pursue and as citizens of a technological society (National Academy of Engineering, 2001).

The Global Economy

The productivity of local engineering groups can be markedly enhanced by globally dispersed "round-the-clock" engineering teams.

Conversely, the disparity in wages may make outsourcing of engineering jobs the dominant feature of global connectivity. Other nations may learn from the lessons of China and India that educating their young people as engineers provides a ready pool of talent to be employed at home in engineering jobs outsourced from the high-wage-cost developed countries. In the United States this may have a chilling effect on domestic job opportunities. Alternatively, in the long run it may increase the buying power of the developing world and vastly increase the total market for U.S. goods and services.

If the demand for U.S. engineers drops, even if only temporarily while the world adjusts to a new economic order, will it be necessary for the traditional engineering schools to develop a two-tiered engineering education system? If routine engineering jobs are mostly outsourced, will we educate large numbers of lower-cost engineering "technicians" to do such jobs? Will U.S. companies be willing to trade off the lower cost of offshore engineers for moderate cost and more local control for engineers at home? Will "full-service" engineers require a five- or six-year "certification" or "professional" degree and act as engineering managers to coordinate the activities of overseas job shops and subsidiaries? What would be the role of ABET (formerly the Accreditation Board for Engineering and Technology, Inc.) in accommodating transition to a professional degree?

If, on the other hand, the demand for engineers ultimately increases because of an expanding market, how do we position U.S. engineers to be prepared? Do our engineers understand enough culturally, for example, to respond to the needs of the multiple niches in a global market? Can we continue to expect everyone else to speak English? What will be our special value added?

The Five- or Six-Year Professional Degree

Almost all discussion of educating the engineer of 2020 presumes additions to the curriculum—more on communications, more of the social sciences, more on business and economics, more cross-cultural studies, more on nano-, bio-, and information technologies, more on the fundamentals behind these increasingly central technologies, and so forth. Unfortunately, the typical undergraduate engineering program already requires around 10 percent more coursework than other degree programs, and a typical engineering student needs 4.8 years to complete it. Simply adding these new elements to the curriculum is not an option.

The options would seem to be: (a) cutting out some of the current requirements, (b) restructuring current courses to teach them much more efficiently, or (c) increasing the time spent in school to become an engineering professional. All three may need to be done to some extent, but it is worth noting that all professions except engineering—business, law, medicine—presume that the bachelor's degree is *not* the first professional degree. They presume the first professional degree is preceded by a nonspecialist liberal arts degree, so it is also not clear that just adding two years or so to a traditional engineering B.S. degree will raise engineers to the professional status of managers, lawyers, and doctors. Nonetheless, while it cannot be mandated instantly and could require radical restructuring of the present approach to engineering education, by 2020 engineering could well follow the course of the other professions. Doing so may be part of the competitive edge of U.S. engineers.

Immigration and the Next Generation of U.S. Engineering Students

In the face of ongoing concerns about terrorism, the United States may permit immigration at only a very carefully metered trickle. This could seriously depress the supply of foreign students and engineers and, in a scenario the opposite of those above, increase the need for engineering schools to recruit, nurture, and retain domestic students. Under the best of circumstances, most engineering schools do not "nurture and retain" particularly well, and the need to do so could be a serious challenge in an "insular" United States.

Decreases in immigration could also severely deplete the pool of foreign graduate students on which the U.S. research "engine" depends so heavily to conduct research in academic settings and to serve as teaching assistants. In the face of the opportunity costs associated with continued schooling, U.S. students exhibit considerable reluctance to pursue the Ph.D. The engineering education establishment will need to address the preparation and inducement, perhaps through more generous compensation for teaching and research assistantships, of U.S. students to pursue advanced degrees to keep the engine running.

Building on Past Successes and Failures

Integrating case histories in engineering education would promote a positive professional identity and sense of tradition—things that engineers are often lacking relative to medical doctors, lawyers, and even scientists. Case histories would also point out a variety of ways that social systems (e.g., government, labor unions, cultural norms, or religious world view) or technical infrastructures (e.g., rail and highway systems, telecommunications facilities, or energy limitations) can compromise the success of a seemingly appropriate technical approach. Studying the successes of innovative engineers could help students understand the roots of imagination and innovation.

Education Research

Retention of entering freshmen to completion of their engineering degrees could increase the number of engineers graduating in a given year by as much as 40 percent. Curricular adjustments that engage students in the creativity of engineering early in their engineering education and application of new pedagogical knowledge about the way different people learn have been shown to markedly enhance retention. The engineering education establishment should embrace research in engineering education as a valued activity for engineering faculty as a means to enhance and personalize the connection to undergraduate students. Faculty must understand the variability in how students learn, so they can adapt teaching styles to the learning style most effective for individual students, and prepare students for a lifetime of learning. The National Research Council (2001) report *How People Learn* and the Carnegie Foundation's Preparation for the Professions Program emphasize the need to understand how learning occurs for a particular discipline (Carnegie, 2004). The Carnegie program has sponsored intensive studies on education for the professions of law, engineering, and clergy. Both initiatives stress the need for curriculum developers, cognitive scientists, educational materials developers, and teachers to work with practicing professionals as they create robust strategies for teaching and learning in the various professional disciplines.

Teamwork, Communication, and Public Policy

The engineering profession recognizes that engineers need to work in teams, communicate with multiple audiences, and immerse themselves in public policy debates and will need to do so more effectively in the future. In the face of pressure, especially from state funding agencies, to cut costs by reducing credit hours for the four-year degree, it remains an open question whether engineering education can step up to the challenge of providing a broader education to engineering graduates.

CONCLUSION

Engineering is problem recognition, formulation, and solution. In the next 20 years, engineers and engineering students will be required to use new tools and apply ever-increasing knowledge in expanding engineering disciplines, all while considering societal repercussions and constraints within a complex landscape of old and new ideas. They will be working with diverse teams of engineers and nonengineers to formulate solutions to yet unknown problems. They will increasingly need to address large-scale systems problems. And they and the engineering education infrastructure will likely need to contend with changes in the nature and scale of the engineering workforce. The nation may be forced to make some hard decisions about the national security and international competitiveness implications of excluding immigrant engineers and/or of exporting large numbers of engineering jobs offshore.

Providing engineers of 2020 with exposure to the history of their profession will give them the basis for honing their judgment and critical thinking skills and enhance their professional self-awareness. Successful engineering is defensive engineering, in which solution analysis is proactive and anticipatory. Engineers must consider past lessons and continue to ask questions of other engineers and nonengineering professionals as knowledge expands exponentially. Engineers will be expected to comprehend all that has been established before them and yet adapt to the changes, diversities, and complexities they will encounter. Engineers will be called on to solve ever more difficult problems by forming revolutionary technologies or by applying existing solutions in unique ways.

Engineering will increasingly be applied in ways that achieve synergy between technical and social systems. For example, engineering will help to establish sustainable transportation systems, efficient methods for energy and power delivery, comprehensive telecommunications networks, and cost-effective methods for delivering adequate food and safe drinking water. As these systems are developed and implemented, extensive coordination activities between cities, regions, and nations may be required. Technical systems will leverage all available resources, including human and social infrastructures, to achieve the desired outcomes and to better ensure sustainability. Thus, the engineers of 2020 will be actively involved in political and community arenas. They will understand workforce constraints, and they will recognize the education and training requirements necessary for dealing with customers and the broader public. Engineering will need to expand its reach and thought patterns and political influence if it is to fulfill its potential to help create a better world for our children and grandchildren.

REFERENCES

Bordogna, J. 1997. Making Connections: The Role of Engineers and Engineering Education. The Bridge 27(1):11-16. Available online at: *http://www.nae.edu/nae/naehome.nsf/weblinks/NAEW-4NHMPY?opendocument*.

Carnegie Foundation for the Advancement of Teaching. 2004. Preparation for the Professions Program Description. Available online at: *http://www.carnegiefoundation.org/ppp*.

Central Intelligence Agency. 2001. Long-Term Global Demographic Trends: Reshaping the Geopolitical Landscape. Available online at: *http://www.odci.gov/cia/reports/Demo_Trends_For_Web.pdf*.

Ehler, V.J. 2003. Presentation at U.S. Congress National Outreach Day, Washington, D.C., September 9.

Fruchter, R. 2002. Interdisciplinary Communications Medium. Available online at: *http://www-cdr.stanford.edu/ICM/icm.html*.

Graham, L.R. 1993. The Ghost of the Executed Engineer: Technology and the Fall of the Soviet Union. Cambridge, Mass.: Harvard University Press.

Lee, R., and J. Haaga. 2002. Government Spending in an Older America. Population Reference Bureau Reports on America, 3(1). Available online at: *http://www.prb.org/Content/NavigationMenu/PRB/PRB_Library/Reports_on_America1/Reports_on_America.htm*.

National Academy of Engineering. 2001. Why All Americans Need to Know More About Technology. Washington, D.C.: National Academy Press.

National Research Council. 2001. How People Learn. Washington, D.C.: National Academy Press.

Shuman, L., C. Atman, E. Eschenbach, D. Evans, R.M. Felder, P.K. Imbrie, J. McGourty, R.L. Miller, L.G. Richards, K.A. Smith, E.P. Soulsby, A.A. Waller, and C.F. Yokomoto. 2002. The Future of Engineering Education. 32nd ASEE/IEEE Frontiers in Education Conference, Boston, Mass., November 6-9.

Smerdon, E. 2003. Global Challenges for U.S. Engineering Education. 6th WFEO World

Congress on Engineering Education, Nashville, Tenn., June 20-23.

Smith, K.A. 2003. Teamwork and Project Management, 2nd Edition. New York: McGraw-Hill.

Tersine, R., and M. Harvey. 1998. Global Customerization of Markets Has Arrived. European Management Journal 16(1):45-57. Available online at: *http://www.ou.edu/class/ tersine/mgt5053/readings/Mgt5053r03.pdf.*

U.S. Census Bureau. 2002. U.S. Census Bureau National Population Projections. Available online at: *www.census.gov/population/www/projections/natproj.html.*

United Nations. 2002. World Urbanization Prospects: The 2001 Revision Data Tables and Highlights. United Nations Department of Economics and Social Affairs, Population Division, New York.

Wind, J., and A. Rangaswamy. 2000. Customerization: The Next Revolution in Mass Customization. eBusiness Research Center, Pennsylvania State University, University Park. Available online at: *http://www.smeal.psu.edu/ebrc/publications/res_papers/ 1999_06.pdf.*

3

Aspirations for the Engineer of 2020

Throughout the ages humankind has sought to divine the future, in the past by consulting the Delphic oracle, today by creating massive computer models. However, life has a habit of reminding us that our predictions are rarely accurate. Despite the fickle nature of events over time, two constants persist. One is that we continue to prepare ourselves for an uncertain future as we always have, and the second is a steady growth of the influence of technology in our lives.

Engineering, through its role in the creation and implementation of technology, has been a key force in the improvement of our economic well-being, health, and quality of life. Three hundred years ago the average life span was 37 years, the primary effort of the majority of humans was focused on provisioning their tables, and the threat of sudden demise due to disease was a lurking reality (Kagan et al., 2001). Today, human life expectancy is approaching 80 years in many parts of the world as fundamental advances in medicine and technology have greatly suppressed the occurrence of and mortality rates for previously fatal diseases and the efforts of humankind are focused largely on enhanced quality of life (Central Intelligence Agency, 2001). Only 150 years ago travel from the East Coast of the United States to the West Coast entailed a hazardous journey that took months to accomplish. Weeks were needed to transmit a letter from one coast to the other. Today, in the developed world, we take it for granted that transportation is affordable and reliable, good health care is accessible, information and entertainment are provided on call, and safe water and healthy food are readily available.

To be sure, there have also been negative results of technology. Pollution, global warming, depletion of scarce resources, and catastrophic failures of poorly designed engineering systems are examples. Overall, however, engineers and their inventions and innovations have helped shape the changes that have made our lives more productive and fruitful.

With the prospect of the exciting new developments expected to come from such fields as biotechnology, nanotechnology, and high-performance computing, the year 2020 can be a time of new choices and opportunities. The years between the present and 2020 offer engineering the opportunity to strengthen its leadership role in society and to define an engineering career as one of the most influential and valuable in society and one that is attractive for the best and the brightest. If we are to take full advantage of this opportunity, it is important to engage all segments of the population in a vigorous discussion of the roles of engineers and engineering and to establish high aspirations for engineers that reflect a shared vision of the future.

VISIONS OF THE COMMITTEE

Our Image and the Profession

Without engineers working both in technical endeavors and as leaders who serve in industry, government, education, and nonprofit organizations, progress would stagnate. Engineering offers men and women an unparalleled opportunity to experience the joy of improving the quality of life for humankind through development of engineering solutions to societal problems. Many engineers pursue career paths in fields that are traditionally defined as engineering. However, a significant number use their engineering backgrounds as points of departure into other fields such as law, medicine, and business. The opportunities offered by an engineering education are multifold, and this is not fully realized by young people, their parents, counselors, mentors, and the public at large.

By 2020, we aspire to a public that will understand and appreciate the profound impact of the engineering profession on sociocultural systems, the full spectrum of career opportunities accessible through

an engineering education, and the value of an engineering education to engineers working successfully in nonengineering jobs.

While engineering is a rapidly evolving field that adapts to new knowledge, new technology, and the needs of society, it also draws on distinct roots that go back to the origins of civilization. Maintaining a linkage of the past with the future is fundamental to the rational and fact-based approaches that engineers use in identifying and confronting the most difficult issues.

We aspire to a public that will recognize the union of professionalism, technical knowledge, social and historical awareness, and traditions that serve to make engineers competent to address the world's complex and changing challenges.

Engineering must be grounded in the fundamental principles of science and mathematics. This foundation supports the development of new knowledge and the creation of safe, reliable, and innovative technologies that advance society and the human condition. Solutions of societal problems require that these technologies be applied in innovative ways with consideration of cultural differences, historical perspectives, and legal and economic constraints, among other issues.

We aspire to engineers in 2020 who will remain well grounded in the basics of mathematics and science, and who will expand their vision of design through a solid grounding in the humanities, social sciences, and economics. Emphasis on the creative process will allow more effective leadership in the development and application of next-generation technologies to problems of the future.

Engineering Without Boundaries

Engineering has shown itself to be responsive to technological breakthroughs from within engineering and from other fields, although not always in the most timely fashion. From its first two subbranches, military and civil, it expanded early on in recognition of developments that led to mining, mechanical, chemical, electrical, and industrial engineering. This process has continued and is evidenced recently by the introduction of biomedical and computer engineering.

We aspire to an engineering profession that will rapidly embrace the potentialities offered by creativity, invention, and cross-disciplinary fertilization to create and accommodate new fields of endeavor, including those that require openness to interdisciplinary efforts with nonengineering disciplines such as science, social science, and business.

With technology becoming ever more pervasive in society, it is incumbent on the engineering profession to lead in shaping the ultimate use of technology and the government processes that control, regulate, or encourage its use.

By 2020 we aspire to engineers who will assume leadership positions from which they can serve as positive influences in the making of public policy and in the administration of government and industry.

The success of engineering is based on a deep reservoir of talented people. In the United States this wellspring has been nourished principally by drawing from a white male population.

We aspire to an engineering profession that will effectively recruit, nurture, and welcome underrepresented groups to its ranks.

Engineering a Sustainable Society and World

The world faces significant environmental challenges in the future. At the same time there is great opportunity for engineering to serve as a force to help society solve the problems associated with these challenges. This requires a holistic understanding of economic growth and development in terms of the principles of sustainability. The present generation has the obligation to leave a legacy to those who follow so they can have the opportunity to appreciate the unrestrained beauty of nature, the full diversity of the world's flora and fauna, and ancient and modern cultures and their artifacts.

It is our aspiration that engineers will continue to be leaders in the movement toward use of wise, informed, and economical sustainable

development. This should begin in our educational institutions and be founded in the basic tenets of the engineering profession and its actions.

Advances in communications, travel, and economics have created a world where no country is untouched by any other. In the United States the oceans that bound our coasts no longer insulate us from other nations. In this dynamic global economy and political environment, engineering must adjust to a new world view.

We aspire to a future where engineers are prepared to adapt to changes in global forces and trends and to ethically assist the world in creating a balance in the standard of living for developing and developed countries alike.

Education of the Engineer of 2020

Engineering education and its nature have been debated for many years. Change typically comes in waves, often following from forces outside the education establishment. Fallout from the surprising success of the launch of the Russian satellite *Sputnik* led to reinforcement of the "engineering science" paradigm. The impacts of the recession of the early 1980s and subsequent reconstitution of the competitiveness of American industry and the dramatic failure of the space shuttle *Challenger* in the mid-1980s aided the movement toward more attention to quality principles and communication and teamwork skills. Presently, it is important that engineering education be reconsidered in a futures-based approach driven from within engineering.

It is our aspiration that engineering educators and practicing engineers together undertake a proactive effort to prepare engineering education to address the technology and societal challenges and opportunities of the future. With appropriate thought and consideration, and using new strategic planning tools, we should reconstitute engineering curricula and related educational programs to prepare today's engineers for the careers of the future, with due recognition of the rapid pace of change in the world and its intrinsic lack of predictability.

It is appropriate that engineers are educated to understand and appreciate history, philosophy, culture, and the arts, along with the creative elements of all of these disciplines. The balanced inclusion of these important aspects in an engineering education leads to men and women who can bridge the "two cultures" cited by the author C.P. Snow (1998). In our increasingly technological society, this is more important now than in the 1950s when Snow identified the issue. The case can be made that an appropriately designed engineering curriculum today offers an education that is more well rounded than that obtained by students majoring in classical liberal arts, where technology is conspicuously absent from the field of study.

Our aspiration is to shape the engineering curriculum for 2020 so as to be responsive to the disparate learning styles of different student populations and attractive for all those seeking a full and well-rounded education that prepares a person for a creative and productive life and positions of leadership.

REFERENCES

Central Intelligence Agency. 2001. Long-Term Global Demographic Trends: Reshaping the Geopolitical Landscape. Available online at: *http://www.odci.gov/cia/reports/Demo_Trends_For_Web.pdf.*

Kagan, D., S. Ozment, and F.M. Turner. 2001. The Western Heritage, 7th Edition. Englewood Cliffs, N.J.: Prentice Hall.

Snow, C.P. 1998. The Two Cultures. Cambridge, United Kingdom: Cambridge University Press.

4

Attributes of Engineers in 2020

We complete our discussion of the engineer of 2020 by reviewing the key attributes that will support the success and relevance of the engineering profession in 2020 and beyond. Our discussion is framed by certain guiding principles that will shape engineering activities, as follows:

- The pace of technological innovation will continue to be rapid (most likely accelerating).
- The world in which technology will be deployed will be intensely globally interconnected.
- The population of individuals who are involved with or affected by technology (e.g., designers, manufacturers, distributors, users) will be increasingly diverse and multidisciplinary.
- Social, cultural, political, and economic forces will continue to shape and affect the success of technological innovation.
- The presence of technology in our everyday lives will be seamless, transparent, and more significant than ever.

CONNECTIONS BETWEEN ENGINEERING PAST, PRESENT, AND FUTURE

Many of the key attributes of engineers in 2020 will be similar to those of today but made more complex by the impact of new technology. In reviewing these enduring attributes for engineers, we also identify the essential characteristics that connect engineering's past, present, and future. As with any profession, we also recognize the imperative to remain flexible and to embrace necessary changes that allow for constant success. These new-century reflections on engineers in 2020 are outlined below.

The word *engineer* has its roots in the Latin word *ingeniator*, which means ingenious, to devise in the sense of construct, or craftsmanship. Several other words are related to ingeniator, including *ingenuity*.

Engineers in 2020, like engineers of yesterday and today, will possess **strong analytical skills**. At its core, engineering employs principles of science, mathematics, and domains of discovery and design to a particular challenge and for a practical purpose. This will not change as we move forward. It has been stated in earlier sections that the core knowledge base on which engineers develop products and services may shift as technologies involving the life sciences, nanoscience, optical science, materials science, and complex systems become more prevalent. Also, information and communications technologies will be ubiquitous—embedded into virtually every structure and process and vital to the success and usefulness of all engineered products. Just as important will be the imperative to expand the engineering design space such that the impacts of social systems and their associated constraints are afforded as much attention as economic, legal, and political constraints (e.g., resource management, standards, accountability requirements). Engineers will also concentrate on systemic outcomes in the same ways that focused outcomes are considered. Even though the scientific knowledge that defines operating principles is expected to be more fluid and more complex, the core analysis activities of engineering design—establishing structure, planning, evaluating performance, and aligning outcomes to a desired objective—will continue.

Engineers in 2020 will exhibit **practical ingenuity**. The word *engineering* derives from *ingeniator* (Johnston et al., 2000). Yesterday, today, and forever, engineering will be synonymous with ingenuity—skill in planning, combining, and adapting. Using science and practical ingenuity, engineers identify problems and find solutions. This will continue to be a mainstay of engineering. But as technology continues to increase in complexity and the world becomes ever more dependent on technology, the magnitude, scope, and impact of the challenges society will face in the future are likely to change. For example, issues related to climate change, the environment, and the intersections between technology and social/public policies are becoming increasingly important. By 2020 the need for practical solutions will be at or near critical stage, and engineers, and their ingenuity, will become ever more important.

Creativity (invention, innovation, thinking outside the box, art) is an indispensable quality for engineering, and given the growing scope of the challenges ahead and the complexity and diversity of the technologies of the 21st century, creativity will grow in importance. The creativity requisite for engineering will change only in the sense that the problems to be solved may require synthesis of a broader range of interdisciplinary knowledge and a greater focus on systemic constructs and outcomes.

As always, good engineering will require good **communication**. Engineering has always engaged multiple stakeholders—government, private industry, and the public. In the new century the parties that engineering ties together will increasingly involve interdisciplinary teams, globally diverse team members, public officials, and a global customer base. We envision a world where communication is enabled by an ability to listen effectively as well as to communicate through oral, visual, and written mechanisms. Modern advances in technology will necessitate the effective use of virtual communication tools. The increasing imperative for accountability will necessitate an ability to communicate convincingly and to shape the opinions and attitudes of other engineers and the public.

In the past those engineers who mastered the principles of **business and management** were rewarded with leadership roles. This will be no different in the future. However, with the growing interdependence between technology and the economic and social foundations of modern society, there will be an increasing number of opportunities for engineers to exercise their potential as leaders, not only in business but also in the nonprofit and government sectors. Policy decisions in technological societies will demand the attention of leaders who understand the strengths and limitations of science and technology. New levels of sophistication will be needed as choices that affect physical, human, and political infrastructures and decisions that define priorities and objectives for a community, region, or nation are made.

In preparation for this opportunity, engineers must understand the principles of **leadership** and be able to practice them in growing proportions as their careers advance. They must also be willing to acknowledge the significance and importance of public service and its place in society, stretching their traditional comfort zone and accepting the challenge of bridging public policy and technology well beyond the roles accepted in the past.

Complementary to the necessity for strong leadership ability is the need to also possess a working framework upon which **high ethical standards** and a strong sense of **professionalism** can be developed. These are supported by boldness and courage. Many of the challenges of the new century are complex and interdependent and have significant implications for the technologies intended to address them and the ways in which those technologies affect the planet and the people that live here. Effective and wise management of technological resources is integral to engineering work. The choices will be gray in nature, balancing (for example) economic, social, environmental, and military factors. Leaders, and those who influence these choices, will benefit from a sense of purpose and clarity. Successful engineers in 2020 will, as they always have, recognize the broader contexts that are intertwined in technology and its application in society.

Given the uncertain and changing character of the world in which 2020 engineers will work, engineers will need something that cannot be described in a single word. It involves **dynamism, agility, resilience, and flexibility**. Not only will technology change quickly, the social-political-economic world in which engineers work will change continuously. In this context it will not be this or that particular knowledge that engineers will need but rather the ability to learn new things quickly and the ability to apply knowledge to new problems and new contexts.

Encompassed in this theme is the imperative for engineers to be **lifelong learners**. They will need this not only because technology will change quickly but also because the career trajectories of engineers will take on many more directions—directions that include different parts of the world and different types of challenges and that engage different types of people and objectives. Hence, to be individually/personally successful, the engineer of 2020 will learn continuously throughout his or her career, not just about engineering but also about history, politics, business, and so forth.

What attributes will the engineer of 2020 have? He or she will aspire to have the ingenuity of Lillian Gilbreth, the problem-solving capabilities of Gordon Moore, the scientific insight of Albert Einstein, the creativity of Pablo Picasso, the determination of the Wright brothers, the leadership abilities of Bill Gates, the conscience of Eleanor Roosevelt, the vision of Martin Luther King, and the curiosity and wonder of our grandchildren.

Lillian Gilbreth is known as the Mother of Ergonomics, a branch of engineering devoted to fitting the workplace to the worker. Ergonomics involves the application of knowledge about human capacities and limitations to the design of workplaces, jobs, tasks, tools, equipment, and the environment. Gilbreth's approach transformed the engineering activity by introducing a primary focus on human needs and capacities. She was recognized for her contributions by being the first woman elected to the National Academy of Engineering in 1966.

REFERENCE

Johnston, S., Gostelow, J.P., and W.J. King. 2000. Engineering and Society. New York: Prentice Hall.

Epilogue

The engineer of 2020 and beyond will face a bewildering array of new technologies, appearing at a rate that will bring his or her professional qualifications constantly near obsolescence. The engineering community will face a world which is more connected than today, requiring both social and political acumen to navigate the changing world conditions. The particular factors that will dominate engineering practice and require reform of engineering education are not predictable, although an array of possible factors is already evident. This report lays out those factors the committee deemed most plausible to have an impact and thus creates a framework of issues that it believes must be considered in a discussion of the action steps for engineering education. That discussion is the subject of Phase II of this project.

A vision of the future engineer is provided by the aspirations and attributes listed in Chapters 3 and 4. These aspirations describe engineers who are broadly educated, see themselves as global citizens, can lead in business and public service, as well as in research, development and design, are ethical and inclusive of all segments of society. The attributes include strong analytical skills, creativity, ingenuity, professionalism, and leadership. We believe that engineers meet these aspirations and evidence these attributes today. The issue is how we can ensure that the engineering profession and engineering education adopt a collective vision including these aspirations and encouraging creation of an environment that promotes these attributes and aspirations in the future.

Appendixes

Appendix A

Scenarios

SCENARIOS

This appendix contains the scenarios referred to in the Preface and Executive Summary. The participants listed in Appendix B developed them at a fall 2002 workshop.

About Scenario Thinking

Scenario planning is a highly interactive process that is intense and imaginative. The idea of scenarios is to tell possible stories about the future. A scenario is a tool for ordering one's perceptions about alternative future environments in which today's decisions might be played out.

The initial phase usually involves rigorously challenging the mental maps that shape one's perceptions. A good scenario planning project expands our peripheral vision and forces us to examine our assumptions and to practice what we would do if the unthinkable happened—a condition that occurs more often than one might imagine.

In the body of the process, groups identify driving forces (social, economic, political, and technological) and the factors that shape those forces. These factors are then prioritized according to importance and uncertainty.

Each scenario should represent a plausible alternative future, not a best case, worst case, or most likely continuum. Most important, the test of a good scenario is not whether it portrays the future accurately but whether it provides a mechanism for learning and adapting.

THE NEXT SCIENTIFIC REVOLUTION

Context

In the past few years we have discovered that the universe is expanding at an accelerating rate and is probably flat rather than curved. We have found evidence of neutrinos with mass. We have completed the first draft of the human genome and started building the fastest computer to solve even more complex problems in biology. In physics, profound changes in our understanding are unfolding at the very large scale of the universe and at the very small scale inside subatomic particles. One of the most challenging problems in physics today is the apparent incompatibility between general relativity, which describes the nature of the large-scale universe very well, and quantum mechanics, which is useful at the very small scale. Like physics, chemistry is benefiting from new computational methods and the ability to manipulate matter at the very small scale. We can simulate chemical reactions and structures that enable us to try many more alternatives in virtual labs than we could ever do in the real world. Research proceeds faster and better. We have new tools to see and manipulate individual molecules. In biology the revolutionary dynamics are similar, with the added dimension of the decoding of the human genome. Advances over the past few decades in genetics and molecular biology have enormously expanded our understanding and control of biological systems. Once biology was mainly an empirical science. We could only observe what is. Unlike physics, we could not reliably predict and control the behavior of systems. Increasingly biology is becoming a quantitative science like physics, with higher levels of ability to predict and control.

We imagine that the new ideas and discoveries in physics, biology, chemistry, and mathematics are leading to a revolutionary "moment" where we will reconceptualize and reperceive reality. We have been here before. One of the consequences of the revolution in physics at the beginning of the 20th century was that reality got weird. In the 19th century, physics made the world more comprehensible. It was assumed that the real world was like a vast clock mechanism. If we identified all its pieces and figured out how they worked, we would understand the nature of things. It was not hard to visualize the causal cascade of events that explained why things are as they are. Then along came relativity and quantum theory. Suddenly space and time became malleable and fluid rather than the fixed framework within which everything else happened. Heisenberg showed us that, thanks to the dynamics of very small things, it was impossible to know just where a particle was and how fast it was moving in what direction. Uncertainty is in the nature of things. We now have great difficulty in imagining the workings of physical reality. After all, can anyone really imagine the big bang . . . a unique discontinuity in the fabric of space-time that suddenly blew up in an explosion of vast energy to create our universe?

In the West, one of the earliest models of the universe was that of Ptolemy. It worked fairly well, except for the fact that it assumed the earth was at the center of the universe and everything rotated around us. As astronomy got more sophisticated, we had to invent ever more elaborate mathematical models to make Ptolemy's picture of reality work. The astral cycles of heavenly movement became cycles within cycles within cycles. Until finally Copernicus said it would all be much simpler if the sun were at the center and we went around it. The way we imagined the workings of the universe literally shifted and it was simple again in both perception and mathematics.

The present moment in science has the whiff of Ptolemeic epicycles about it. Perhaps the universe is actually incredibly complex and incomprehensible. Or just maybe it is our models that have become complex and incomprehensible. Perhaps the new theories will yield ways of seeing things that are not as simpleminded as the clockwork universe of the 19th century or as illusive as the unimaginable world of the 20th century. In our new understandings of the relationship of the very large to the very small we may literally revisualize the universe around us.

New Tools

Scientific advances often rely on the engineering of new tools to open new arenas for exploration. The telescope and the microscope changed our view of the very large and the very small. Atom smashers, now called particle accelerators, made it possible to explore the interior of the atom. X-ray crystallography made possible the discovery of the double helix of the DNA molecule.

Today new scientific tools are leading to profound insights into the realities of nature. The Hubble telescope and other space-based as well as terrestrial astronomical instruments have taken us almost all the way to the edge of the universe and back to its origins in the big bang. Over the coming decade we anticipate building several huge new telescopes both on the ground and in space. The scanning tunneling microscope has given us the ability to see and manipulate individual atoms. New imaging techniques have allowed us to observe the dynamics of very fast chemical reactions.

The most important new tool, however, has been the computer. It has given us the ability to create remarkably faithful simulations of phenomena like turbulent flow and complex chemical reactions. It has allowed us to study very large numbers of examples, millions instead of dozens. It has given us the control systems to manipulate very complex and/or microscopic processes. Indeed, hard scientific problems continue to help advance the frontiers of computing power. Using today's supercomputers already allows us to simulate many thousands of potential chemical reactions and focus on the most productive few to test on the lab bench. IBM is currently building the world's most powerful computer, to be known as Blue Gene, to simulate the complex three-dimensional geometry and dynamics of protein molecules.

The Internet, of course, was primarily a tool for accelerating scientific communication. It used to be that the process of research involved a long cycle of peer review, publishing, challenging, retesting, publishing, and so on. It was a process that took months or even years. Today an experiment is conducted in the morning, and the results can be on the Internet by lunchtime. By midafternoon they might be validated elsewhere in the world and confirmed by the end of the day.

Ideas can be key tools, too. An important new idea has emerged in recent years—the mathematics of chaos. A whole new way of seeing change in evolving systems has been rigorously described by this new mathematical discipline. Two new principles of change emerge from chaos theory. Small changes at the beginning of a process of evolution can have very large effects much further downstream. Second, the outcome of a process is dependent on the path it took to get there. Small, almost random changes accumulate over time to make the developmental path of every system in nature unique, if only slightly. On every tree the leaves are very similar but not identical. In the universe there are many spiral galaxies, but none duplicate our own Milky Way galaxy.

Their uniqueness is a function of all the unique events along the way for each system that add up to a slightly different shape and size for the leaf and the galaxy.

A Broad, Deep Revolution

Part of what makes one imagine that a revolution is coming is that fundamental changes are developing across many disciplines. Here the focus is on physics, biology, and chemistry, but many others could be covered. Furthermore, they are feeding on each other.

The powerful new tools of astronomy and astrophysics, which include not only the Hubble and other huge ground-based telescopes like the Keck, but also instruments that explore in other spectra like x-ray, gamma-ray, and radio, are leading to often surprising discoveries. Among other things we have found that the universe is expanding at an accelerating rate rather than a constant or decelerating rate. This challenges our model of the composition of the universe. Some unknown force is causing the acceleration. The new discoveries are forcing us to reconsider our models of the very large-scale universe.

At the other end of the scale, new findings in particle research and theories like superstrings are leading to revisions of our ever more subtle model of the subatomic realm. Indeed, superstring theory has the potential to be the idea that breaks through the dilemma of the conflict between relativity and quantum theory. It may be the unifying theory of everything. (For a good book on the subject, see Brian Greene's *The Elegant Universe,* Vintage Publishing, 2000.)

In the new physics there are also hints of what could become technologically possible. Certainly superconductivity at room temperature seems plausible. New ways of transforming energy also seem plausible. The chemistry that lies ahead will have two new distinct properties. We are increasingly going to be able to predict the dynamics of chemical reactions and the properties of the resulting new materials using computational methods. It means that we will be able to design new materials never before seen. In the current research on carbon nanotubes, we are already seeing this process at work. Second, we will have much greater fine grain control of molecular dynamics and structures. We are going to be able to maneuver molecules for many purposes from testing to molecular construction. So the new materials we invent on the computer we will actually be able to make. The revolution lies in the movement of chemistry from the realm of vast numbers of molecules colliding at random to a chemistry that treats individual molecules as meaningful entities. Imagine building with Legos rather than making soup.

In biology the revolution lies in being able to understand the myriad biological processes and structures that shape our world and lives. Among the key outcomes, of course, will be radical new medical therapies, from being able to grow custom replacement tissue to curing most diseases and even reversing aging.

The intersection of the new physics, chemistry, and biology is in nanoscience and technology. The idea is to make functional devices at the atomic and molecular scales. A variety of biological molecules and systems provide useful models. In the new understanding of chemistry we are learning how to align and manipulate molecules in new ways. In the new physics we are gaining insight into the nature of the atoms themselves. The results are amazing new devices, for example, sensors that can detect a single molecule in a gas.

When Eric Drexler first articulated his vision of nanotechnology in 1986, most physicists derided it as implausible. Because of the irrepressible movements of very small things, you could never control them or make them stable enough to build nanoscale machines, even if nature did. Fortunately, they were wrong. Nanoscience has moved from the wild fringes of science to the mainstream faster than any idea in history.

The Singularity Scenario

The outcome of these revolutionary dynamics is uncertain. Perhaps the theorists who argue that there is no new revolution are right. It is all the details from here on or we will never figure it out, but in any case the story is mostly over. Well, that is one scenario in which case we are unlikely to be surprised by much in the coming decades. The world of 2020 will mostly resemble today, maybe a bit more technological presence, but no radical departures from the current science and technology.

Or maybe these developments have the potential to be revolutionary but remain quite distinct from each other. They develop over a much longer period and perhaps a century from now will have accumulated into something significant but difficult to glimpse. In any event the world of 2020 is likely to be fairly familiar with only a few surprises along the way. Given what we now know, the surprises are most likely to come in biology. So we could imagine some fairly radical developments such as cures for many diseases and even the beginnings of age reversal and life extension.

But what if these developments are truly revolutionary and they interact to feed on each other along with many other fields to drive an explosive period of change. In part, of course, the drive comes from the high rewards now available for new technology. But ideas, talent, power, and wealth could combine to fuel a revolution in science and technology. It could create a conceptual "singularity," as Vernor Vinge described this moment. It becomes progressively more difficult to imagine the emerging world as the pace and magnitude of change continue to accelerate. Like the Spanish peasant, we may want to hug the ground as the emerging universe whirls around us.

We can imagine the consequences of some of the new world view. We would inhabit a highly interconnected universe in which human action matters but one in which control is extremely difficult. We would have remarkable new capabilities to manufacture new devices and new materials in entirely ecologically benign ways. We might even have new clean energy sources. It would be as different from today as a world of airplanes and automobiles was from the horse and buggy and steamships.

THE BIOTECHNOLOGY REVOLUTION
IN A SOCIETAL CONTEXT

At 9:00 p.m. the alarm from Katherine's internal digital-clock appendage startles her, making her nearly drop the culture she's been working on for the past two hours. After a morning of answering questions from the press, an afternoon of virtual meetings with other scientists in France, home of the world leaders in neuromachines, the only time she can get to make use of her doctorate in biomechanics is late in the evenings. Katherine reluctantly pulls herself from her work and carefully stores the culture so she can finish her experiment in the morning. She removes her lab coat and exits the lab, headed toward her corner office. She passes a line of offices where others are still engrossed in their work. One woman is on the phone setting up meetings with the congressional Bio-Machines Oversight Committee. Another woman tries to finish an article for the *Times* on the company's current research into external uteruses and its potential effects on unborn fetuses and gender inequalities in the workplace. A gentleman is finishing paperwork to be submitted to the company's pro-bono division on the long-term effects of a $40 million donation he oversaw to distribute the AIDS vaccine in Kenya and Zimbabwe.

Katherine slowly walks through the front door. She's tired but decides to not spring for another dose of caffeine. Her vitals monitor tells her that her heart rate is low and her blood sugar and potassium levels are too low—precisely at the right levels for deep REM sleep. She waits impatiently for two minutes as the valet retrieves her car. Before she left her desk, Katherine told her computer via the brain-com interface to have her car waiting for her at the North Lobby. The delay caused by the congressionally mandated requirement that only humans drive cars frustrates her—machines are more reliable and efficient, she thinks to herself. Finally, the valet driving her car arrives. She tips him and then pushes the "home" button on her GPS navigator. The car slowly exits the parking lot. "I'm still pushing buttons," she thinks to herself. If she had the latest model car with the brain-com interface introduced by her company, she wouldn't have to press a button. Ten minutes later she's home.

Katherine unlocks her apartment door via the fingerprint-encoded lock, drops her things, then rushes to the computer to download her thoughts about exactly where she was in the experiment so she can start back up the next day. As her brain is scanned, she also tells her microwave to heat some milk for her to drink to help her off to sleep. Before bed, she prints a copy of the day's newspaper. Though paper is a thing of the past, reading from printed sheets reminds her of her childhood and helps her get to sleep.

"Wednesday, March 15, 2018," she says aloud. "What a day in history!" Five years ago, to the day, marked the beginning of the second attack into Iraq. The Baath Party reemerged to seize the government despite the efforts of the United States and the United Nations to establish democracy following the first war in 2003. Following evidence that new programs to field nuclear, chemical, and biological weapons had emerged, the UN, led by the United States, sent in bombers, followed by ground troops to oust the Baath Party again. Unwilling to yield so quickly this time, party leaders ordered the launch of biological weapons on the U.S. troops and also sent drones over Israel to spray a deadly, genetically modified variant of Ebola that Iraqi scientists were able to develop through advances using stem cells. Ebola-C, as it was called in this country, a powerful virus that could spread through any bodily fluid exchange, would attach itself to vulnerable cells in the body and modify its genetic information such that the cells it would spawn would burst, spreading the virus further through the body until a major organ was destroyed. Death was certain within one to six weeks. Five hundred thousand troops, 79 percent of the troops sent to the Middle East, were killed by the initial release. One million people in Israel were killed. The virus spread through many parts of the Middle East, leading to the deaths of 3.5 million more people within three months.

Galvanized by the threat of a worldwide pandemic, public health organizations around the world focused on finding a cure for the Ebola-C virus. Fortunately for the United States, the disease did not travel to the States. Nevertheless, the public was stunned by the swiftness and scope of the attack and was intent on redoubling efforts to advance the country's knowledge of the life sciences to defend against similar terrorist attacks. To facilitate R&D, a major policy change was made to encourage stem cell research. Shortly thereafter, federal research funds, on par with funds invested during the cold war, were provided specifically for research in the life sciences. Los Alamos, Sandia, and Lawrence Livermore national laboratories and the National Aeronautics and Space Administration developed biological sciences programs, recruiting top researchers, M.D.-Ph.D.s, biologists, chemists, physicists, and engineers to the task of building up America's life sciences know-how. All of the top universities expanded their degree programs in bioengineering—biomechanical, bioelectrical, biochemical engineering. The race for a cure for Ebola-C, and for further advances in life sciences, had begun. In four short months a cure and a vaccine for Ebola-C were developed in France, where researchers had long been doing stem cell research and where many top U.S. scientists had emigrated so they could continue their work in the early 2000s. The United States continued to press fundamental life sciences research and by 2017 was again the world leader in the life sciences arena. Cures and vaccines for AIDS, cancer, anthrax, and most of the other deadly diseases had been developed.

Flush with success but somewhat removed in time from the last warfare/terrorist event, the United States established many governmental oversight committees to monitor and direct research dollars, fueled by religious conservatives still concerned about potential "creation of life" abuses and by antiglobal business activists protesting the profits of U.S. biotechnology companies. Universities began to develop degree programs in ethics, life sciences, and society; courses in biological advances were added to liberal arts programs; and courses in ethics were made requirements in all science and engineering degree programs. By 2017 there were a plethora of bio start-ups and bio products on the market, selling everything from internal vital monitors, weight loss drugs to reprogram the body to stop creating fat cells, memory-enhancing drugs, biomaterial prostheses, and replacement internal organs. The year

2018 brought the release of brain-machine-interacting products, following the huge leaps that had come in understanding the brain and advances in nanotecology and microelectronic mechanical systems. Brain-machine communication devices for computers became commonplace, leading to decreased sales of keyboards. In the homes of those with the highest incomes, it's not uncommon to find the entire home equipped with wireless brain-com controllers for TVs and kitchen appliances.

Katherine sipped her milk and skimmed through the day's national headlines. "Chess Olympiad's Medal Rescinded After Use of Memory Appendage," she reads. "Religious Conservatives Protest Baby-Engineering Research." Not tonight, she thinks to herself. On the education pages she sees the title, "Engineering Schools Recruiting Male Applicants into Life Sciences Careers." She smiles to herself, remembering the late 1990s when men largely dominated engineering classes at most universities. When Katherine entered MIT in 2002, near the beginning of the life sciences boom, she was one of the few women double majoring in physics and biology. She and many of her female classmates sought careers that would have an impact on people's lives and thus chose to enter the bio arena for graduate school. By the time Katherine was in graduate school, the number of women in engineering degree programs equaled that of men nationwide—with many women concentrated in the engineering aspects of the life sciences. Many of her colleagues garnered technical jobs; others became part of the political landscape by joining the staffs of congressional oversight committees; still others engaged in public relations and marketing for the top life sciences companies. Katherine's closest friend in graduate school, Ayodele Amana from Lagos, Nigeria, decided to spend her life getting the advances in life sciences all the way to the poorest migrants in Africa, who badly needed AIDS vaccinations and even the simplest of vitamins and water purification techniques that were commonplace in America generations ago. With the network of people Ayodele had met in graduate school, she was able to start a nonprofit that was largely funded by the larger bio corporations in the States. The disparity between the rich and poor was still growing, but through the work of people like Ayodele the rate was slowing.

The time 9:45 p.m. flashed in Katherine's mind. If she was going to get up early the next morning to get some lab time in before handling the press conference, she would have to get to sleep soon. So she set her alarm for 6:00 a.m., got in bed, told her steamer what outfit she wanted to wear the next day, turned off all the lights in her house, and then laid back and closed her eyes. "After all the life sciences advances of the past 15 years," Katherine thought to herself, "why is it that we haven't figured out an alternative to sleeping?"

THE NATURAL WORLD INTERRUPTS
THE TECHNOLOGY CYCLE

Global Context

In the beginning, at least, Johannesburg proved little different than Rio—high hopes but a disappointing level of global action. In the absence of binding agreements or catalyzing events, the world by 2010 was a natural projection of what existed at the start of the 21st century. There were, to be sure, another 400 million people, and significant increases in cheap computing power had occurred. In "have" countries, that played out into increased visualization and computational abilities that incrementally pushed medicine, engineering, science, and business. Meanwhile, ethical storms over biological manipulation and bio-mechanical hybridization held the public's real attention.

In the other three-fourths of the world, survival remained the dominant imperative. By 2010, developing nations experienced premature deaths of nearly 3 million citizens per year due to inadequate water, food distribution, and power infrastructures. As in the previous decades, unless those deaths fell close together geographically and temporally so that the media could effectively cover a "disaster," little happened. The 400,000 who starved in the Somali drought in 2005 did elicit food aid for East Africa. But sadly, when three times that number died from contaminated water the next year in all of Africa, little happened.

By 2020 advances in many fields held hope for the now 7.1 billion occupants of earth. Genetically altered food had, for better or worse, been accepted in Europe and Africa and starvation was less frequent. Major advances in conservation had taken place in some parts of the world, while others burned their energy with abandon. Petroleum was still the key to transportation and major power plants continued to dominate electricity distribution, though the first real economic inroads of alternative energy sources took hold late in the decade. The predicted ecological collapse had not happened yet. Doomsayers saw dirty water, air, and soil just around the corner, while others declared that earth's systems were far too robust to falter simply because virtually the whole planet was now farmed, lived on, or otherwise used for human purposes.

The world also finally stepped up to the titanic problem of providing clean water for every person every day. The cost was not low, both in disruption and dollars. Water was used in greater harmony with the climate; rice was no longer grown in deserts. And through a concerted effort, low-cost solutions for providing clean water in the poorest regions were paid for and implemented by the G8 (with the help and cooperation of all nations). This effort surpassed all of the more glamorous advances in biotechnology for preserving human life. While breathtaking (and much breath was spent debating their morality), the benefits of cloning and nano-biotechnology were available only in the wealthy portions of the world.

Natural disasters continued at an even pace. AIDS predictably killed 150 million people by 2020, but the epidemic dramatically slowed, as the pool of people infected got smaller. Earthquake abatement strategies continued to be enforced in Japan and California: new buildings were built to code, older buildings were retooled. Hurricane evacuation routes along the Gulf and Florida coasts, along with an increase in the ability to forecast hurricanes, limited human death but not property destruction.

Politically these were turbulent times. Local wars and uprisings seemed endemic. While the Afghan conflict started the century, other hot spots in Asia, Africa, and South America seemed to flare up two or three at a time. As one area found peace or at least a tense calm, it seemed two more wars sprang up. Nothing ever escalated to engulf an entire region—though the 2012 Korean affair easily might have, given the posturing of China and the United States. And the predicted global chaos from a major cyberterrorism attack on the economic system never occurred—though not for lack of trying. Fortunately, so far the security people have stayed just far enough ahead of the terrorists, and the hits that have occurred were best described as disruptive but not devastating.

Natural Disasters

It was a dark and stormy night in Miami. Hurricane Stephan, the fifth category 5 storm to lash Florida in 2011 and the twelfth hurricane of the year, was holding sway on October 10. Yet the damage would not be what it might have been. The reasons are complex, but probably two tell the story best. One is the increased power of computers, and the other was the 2004 United Nations conference on disaster prevention, generally known as the "disaster conference," the recommendations of which Floridians (and residents of Tokyo, Singapore, and most disaster-plagued areas) are happy to have heeded. The conference was the result of insurance company pressures combined with increased abilities to predict severe events and fairly solid predictions of increased natural disasters.

Essentially, the world representatives decided the chances of an increase in the number, severity, and points of landfall for hurricanes were high enough to take preventive actions. Response was primarily of a planning and education nature until a significant improvement in both climate models and cutting-edge computational power combined to give a (relatively) convincing prediction of an oncoming era of many very large hurricanes. At that point, serious money was spent to prepare. By the demonic Atlantic hurricane season of 2011, major hardening of both homes and public infrastructure was a reality. While there is little that can be done about tornadoes imbedded in 125-mph baseline winds, the rise of distributed power in hurricane areas did much to alleviate the scope of power loss. Major public buildings (hospitals, etc.) were upgraded to withstand those winds. Localities equipped community centers with steady supplies of food and water due to regular, if tempo-rary, evacuations. More folks bought generators to share or to use at home. Residents moved out of the lowest areas when it became clear they would be wiped out by storm surges nearly every year and when faced with financial incentives, both positive and negative, that is, the unavailability of low-cost loans to rebuild and tax incentives to move. The net result was a big increase in retirement communities in Arizona and a corresponding decline in Florida. Tourism faded some in Florida, especially from June through December. The state offered tax incentives for low-cost industries to relocate inland.

The "disaster conference" seems to have missed tsunami coverage. Looking back on the 2004 world conference, the one major "mistake" was downgrading to less important efforts to protect against tidal waves. At the time the chances seemed too low and the cost too high. And the asteroid striking the Pacific Ocean in 2017 was certainly a surprise. It didn't fit the "insurance" model; 1.3 million died in the Puget Sound region alone, and the economic cost was in the multiple trillions of dollars in the United States alone (Tokyo did not suffer a direct tidal hit, a blessing that saved 10 million lives).

The almost total destruction of the heart of two major corporations combined with public panic caused the biggest stock market plunge in U.S. history, and, until industry worked out the effects, the whole country suffered. The loss of the ports of Vancouver and Seattle crippled southwestern Canada and the northwestern United States. The grain crop of eastern Washington was partly lost since it could not be shipped. Logging virtually ceased because product could not be shipped. The loss of inland jobs was a surprise addition to the "wave" of depression that followed the wave of water. Virtually everyone in the surrounding 200 miles lost a friend or family member. Psychiatric services were swamped. Suicide levels tripled in Washington.

The collapse of Microsoft and Boeing, combined with the almost total collapse of the insurance industry, plunged financial markets worldwide into a tailspin. Almost overnight, investors opted out of the market—until they could figure out where to put their money, they sat on it. The northwest power grid went down, taking parts of California and Oregon with it. The country did respond: rolling brownouts across the West shared the burden but hurt manufacturing everywhere. Fearing the future, people stopped buying all but the essentials. They didn't leave their homes as often.

The public health system in the Seattle area was a disaster. Beyond the immediate deaths, hundreds of thousands died due to their inability to get treatment or even prescription medicines. Epidemics of cholera and other waterborne diseases were rampant. There was little fresh water, other than what was provided in disaster relief.

Fires from the failure of fuel pipelines, large and small, caused destruction of many buildings that actually survived the wave. To help in the disaster and aid recovery, much of the U.S. military was deployed to the area. Soldiers were the construction workers, road builders, electric power restorers, and food distributors. This use of military personnel immediately reduced the ability of the United States to send forces into the rest of the world and thus reduced the country's ability to fight a foreign threat.

In the ensuing years a great deal of effort went into determining areas of historic vulnerability, methods to passively disrupt Tsunami, and relocation of the most essential institutions. Tidal waves now carry the urgency of their fraternal twins—earthquakes. Seattle is now the model city in this planning. Most property below what is known now as the "high water mark" is devoted to parks and "expendable" uses. All essential services are routed underground. The innovations are innumerable. In the end it was cascading effects that determined the scale of devastation and convinced the world that the cost of preparing for tidal waves was not too high.

Other world events paled in comparison to Seattle's tsunami. In general, the trends of the decade continued. There were no major volcanic eruptions in populated areas. Until Seattle, proposed efforts to protect the few U.S. cities at threat for natural disasters were a constant target for budget trimming.

GLOBAL CONFLICT OR GLOBALIZATION?

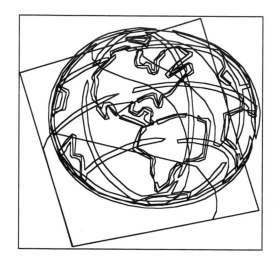

Global Conflict

The Washington bomb went off in 2013. Members of the administration and other world leaders died instantly, reawakening the U.S. populace to the realization that the lull in terrorism in the mainland United States since September 2001 was illusory. The driving factors were little changed over the intervening 12+ years. In the West, economic and societal disparities grew extreme, while in the East pressures from population explosions and religious fundamentalism continued unabated.

The bombardment of the World Trade Center towers in 2001 opened eyes to the increasing technological disparities between the nations. An immediate military response removed that particular group of terrorists, but others saw the attack as a major success and made plans of their own. The ensuing world action taken against Iraq created illusions of peace and prosperity for the next few years, but while economic development returned to breakneck pace, the influences that precipitated the first attack only worsened.

New worries began in 2004 when Pakistan's government was taken over by a group of religious fundamentalists, whose agenda included shaking off the effects of American cultural imperialism. Political and religious alliances in the Middle East sprouted, making it clear that any military action would result in a conflagration of the whole region, thus preventing outside involvement. Tensions grew in the Kashmir region, and a nuclear skirmish was narrowly averted thanks to surprise intervention by the Chinese, where the communist party remains in power to this day. Small-scale terrorism began around the world, and even though many of the attacks were attributed to the new extremist regimes, no efforts were taken to displace them.

After the horrific terrorist attacks at the Olympics in 2008, foreign vacation travel all but ceased, and governments started tightening their borders to prevent future attacks. These protectionist tactics crippled the world economy, reducing trade and ending economic cooperation. The United States saw equal gains in defense spending and its homeless populations; homeland defense and military spending reached half of the receding gross domestic product in 2010. To make matters worse, new restrictions were placed on visas for foreign graduate students and on H-1B visas, bringing university science and engineering research programs to a low ebb and strangling small businesses that could not afford to compete for scarce technical personnel.

To some, terrorism and the military actions to combat it were linked with the availability of technology; thus, in 2020 they found themselves fearing technology and those who wielded it as much as they once loved it. For them, economic, political, and religious beliefs have eclipsed a belief in the value of technology, taking away both the demand and the desire to engineer new devices.

Despite efforts worldwide to close borders, a rise in terrorism appeared in the major economic powers—even Japan and Switzerland saw increased activities, driven as much by a desire to attack sources of technology as by a desire to attack the nation itself. Feelings of nationalism reduced international cooperation. Stuck in their own downward economic spiral, many countries eliminated their aid to Africa and South America. Heightened security led to groups curtailing all efforts to distribute better technologies to third world nations, leading to rampant problems with sanitation and water quality. These events sparked more desperate measures to express anger over the divide between affluent and impoverished societies.

Globalization

In the face of terrorist threats, the developed world moved to isolate the developing world to the degree that it could. Among traditional trading partners, it remained business as usual. While major international companies had long moved manufacturing and technical service jobs overseas in search of low-cost suppliers, the pressure to outsource "creative" jobs, such as engineering design, mounted. This placed severe downward pressure on the availability of engineering jobs in the U.S. economy. Further factors helping to displace jobs for new engineers were the productivity enhancements made possible by computer-aided design and software engineering. A new bimodal class system of engineers emerged: an elite few charged with controlling software improvements and a lesser class of technicians who executed the standard programs and implemented the results. Engineers found few jobs outside the defense industry, and only the major engineering universities survived the downturn in enrollments.

Dangerous concentrations of disaffected young people existed in many developing countries, driven by modest improvements in health care and high birth rates. Those countries with more enlightened leadership recognized that education is a solution and that technology is the engine of growth and thus moved to create or enhance their systems of technical education. The cadres of scientists and engineers created were available for outsourcing of technical jobs from the United States while their indigenous industries were being created.

Appendix B

Workshop Attendees

KEYNOTE PRESENTERS

Philip Condit (NAE)
Chairman and CEO
The Boeing Company

Bran Ferren
Co-chairman and Chief Creative Officer
Applied Minds, Inc.

Shirley A. Jackson (NAE)
President
Rensselaer Polytechnic Institute

Peter Schwartz
Chairman
Global Business Networks

INVITED GUESTS

Richard Y. Chiao
Manager
Ultrasounds Systems Engineering
General Electric Medical Systems

Lloyd S. Cluff (NAE)
Manager
Geosciences Department
Pacific Gas and Electric Company

Connie L. Gutowski
Director (former)
6 Sigma/Truck Business Group
Ford Motor Company

Charles Hura
Engineering Manager
Eastman Kodak Company

Scott W. Jorgensen
Manager
Energy Storage Systems Group
General Motors R&D Center

Karen W. Markus
Vice President
Technology Strategy
JDS Uniphase Corporation

Paul MacCready (NAE)
Chairman
AeroVironment, Inc.

Gary S. May
Executive Assistant to the President
Motorola Foundation Professor of Microelectronics in Electrical and
    Computer Engineering
Office of the President
Georgia Institute of Technology

Pamela McCorduck
Author

Eugene S. Meieran (NAE)
Intel Fellow and Director
Intel Corporation

Jill T. Sideman
Director and Vice President
CH2M HILL

Marvin Theimer
Senior Researcher
Microsoft Research

Rudolph Tromp
Engineering Consultant
Corporate Technical Strategy and Development
IBM Corporation

ENGINEERING STUDENTS

Ron Grover
College of Engineering
University of Michigan

Danielle Hinton
Department of Electrical Engineering
Massachusetts Institute of Technology

Elizabeth Hollenbeck
Department of Mechanical and Aerospace Engineering
University of California at Irvine

Alan J. Michaels
College of Engineering
Georgia Institute of Technology

STEERING COMMITTEE

G. Wayne Clough (NAE), *Chair*
President
Georgia Institute of Technology

Alice M. Agogino (NAE)
Roscoe and Elizabeth Hughes Professor of Mechanical Engineering
University of California, Berkeley

George Campbell, Jr.
President
Cooper Union for the Advancement of Art and Science

James Chavez
Manager
Government Relations
Sandia National Laboratory

David O. Craig
Director
Retail IT—Back Office Applications
Reliant Energy

José B. Cruz, Jr. (NAE)
Howard D. Winbigler Chair in Engineering and Professor of Electrical
    Engineering
The Ohio State University

Peggy Girshman
Broadcast Journalist
National Public Radio

Daniel E. Hastings
Professor of Engineering Systems and Aeronautics and Astronautics
Massachussetts Institute of Technology

Michael J. Heller
Professor
Department of Bioengineering/Electronic Engineering and Computer
    Science
University of California, San Diego

Deborah G. Johnson
Olsson Professor of Applied Ethics
Department of Technology, Culture and Communication
University of Virginia

Alan C. Kay (NAE)
Founder and President
Viewpoints Research Institute

Tarek Khalil
Professor, Department of Industrial Engineering
University of Miami

Robert W. Lucky (NAE)
Corporate Vice President
Telcordia Technologies

John M. Mulvey
Professor, Department of Operations Research and Financial Engineering
Princeton University

Sharon L. Nunes
Vice President, Emerging Businesses
T.J. Watson Research Center
IBM Corporation

Henry Petroski (NAE)
Aleksandar S. Vesic Professor of Civil Engineering and Professor of History
Duke University

Sue V. Rosser
Dean of Ivan Allen College
The Liberal Arts College of Georgia Tech and Professor of History,
    Technology, and Society
Georgia Institute of Technology

Ernest T. Smerdon (NAE)
Emeritus Professor of Civil Engineering and Professor of Hydrology
University of Arizona

NAE STAFF

Wm. A. Wulf (NAE), President
Lance A. Davis (NAE), Executive Officer
Proctor Reid, Associate Director, Program Office
Patricia F. Mead, Senior Program Officer
Matthew E. Caia, Senior Project Assistant

Appendix C

Biographical Sketches of Committee Members

G. WAYNE CLOUGH (chair) is president of the Georgia Institute of Technology and a recognized leader in engineering education and research. A civil engineer, he holds bachelor's and master's degrees from Georgia Tech and a Ph.D. from the University of California, Berkeley. He served on the faculties of Stanford and Duke universities before becoming head of the civil engineering department and then dean of the College of Engineering at Virginia Polytechnic Institute and State University. Prior to returning to his alma mater as president, he was provost and vice president for academic affairs at the University of Washington. His professional expertise in geotechnical and earthquake engineering is reflected in the 120 papers and reports and six book chapters he has published. He has consulted with 60 firms and boards and is presently a special consultant to San Francisco's Bay Area Rapid Transit for ongoing major seismic retrofit operations. His broader interests include technology and higher education policy, economic development, diversity in higher education, and technology in a global setting. In 2001, President George W. Bush appointed Dr. Clough to the President's Council of Advisors on Science and Technology, and he chairs the panel on federal research and development. He is also a member of the executive committee of the U.S. Council on Competitiveness. He received the 2001 National Engineering Award from the American Association of Engineering Societies, and the American Society of Civil Engineers has recognized him with seven national awards. He is one of the few to have been twice honored with civil engineering's oldest award, the Norman Medal. He was elected to the National Academy of Engineering in 1990.

ALICE M. AGOGINO is the Roscoe and Elizabeth Hughes Professor of Mechanical Engineering and directs several computational and design research and instructional laboratories at the University of California (UC), Berkeley. She received a B.S. in mechanical engineering from the University of New Mexico, an M.S. in mechanical engineering in 1978 from UC Berkeley, and a Ph.D. from the Department of Engineering-Economic Systems at Stanford University in 1984. She has authored over 120 scholarly publications in the areas of microelectronic mechanical systems/mechatronics design methods; nonlinear optimization; intelligent learning systems; multiobjective and strategic product design; probabilistic modeling; intelligent control and manufacturing; graphics, multimedia, and computer-aided design; design databases; digital libraries; artificial intelligence and decision and expert systems; and gender and technology. She has won numerous teaching, best paper, and research awards. Dr. Agogino is known internationally as a leader in engineering education and is a member of the National Academy of Engineering's Committee on Engineering Education. She served as director for Synthesis, a National Science Foundation/industry-sponsored coalition of eight universities with the goal of reforming undergraduate engineering education, and continues as principal investigator for the NEEDS (*www.needs.org*) and *SMETE.ORG* digital libraries of courseware in science, mathematics, engineering, and technology. Dr. Agogino has also served in a number of administrative positions at UC Berkeley, including associate dean of engineering, director of the Instructional Technology Program, and faculty assistant to the executive vice chancellor and provost in educational development and technology. Professor Agogino is a registered professional mechanical engineer in California and is engaged in a number of collaborative projects with industry. Prior to joining the faculty at UC Berkeley, she worked in industry for Dow Chemical, General Electric, and SRI International.

GEORGE CAMPBELL, JR., is president of The Cooper Union for the Advancement of Science and Art, one of America's most selective institutions of higher education. Previously, Dr. Campbell served as president and chief executive officer of NACME, Inc., and in various R&D and management positions at AT&T Bell Laboratories. Earlier in his career, Dr. Campbell served on the faculties of Syracuse University and Nkumbi International College in Zambia. He has published numerous papers and is coeditor of *Access Denied: Race, Ethnicity and the Scientific Enterprise* (Oxford University Press, Oxford, 2000). Dr. Campbell currently serves on the board of directors of Consolidated Edison, Inc., and as a trustee of Rensselaer Polytechnic Institute, Montefiore Medical Center, and the New York Hall of Science. He has also served on a number of science and technology policy bodies, including the Morella Commission of the U.S. Congress, the U.S. Secretary of Energy's Advisory Board, National Research Council committees and as chair of the New York City Chancellor's Task Force on Science Education. Among his many awards are two honorary doctorates. A graduate of the Executive Management Program at Yale University, Dr. Campbell earned a Ph.D. in theoretical physics from Syracuse University and a B.S. in physics from Drexel University, where he was a Simon Guggenheim Scholar.

JAMES CHAVEZ, prior to being awarded an American Society of Mechanical Engineers (ASME) federal government fellowship, was manager of Sandia National Laboratories government relations organization. In this position he worked closely with Sandia's leadership and Congress to address national issues on energy, weapons stewardship, and science and technology. Chavez has also participated in the research, development, and demonstration of renewable technologies for utility applications. His responsibilities included managing the activities for the Department of Energy's Concentrating Solar Power Program and Biomass Power and Solar Buildings Program. He also served as manager of the National Solar Thermal Test Facility at Sandia National Laboratories (Albuquerque), the largest solar test facility in the United States. He contributed to the conception, development, construction, and testing of the world's largest solar power plant, the 10 MWe Solar Two Power Plant in Barstow, California. Chavez earned his bachelor's and master's degrees in mechanical engineering from New Mexico State University, Las Cruces, in 1981, and the University of California, Berkeley, in 1982, respectively. In 1997 he was named recipient of the Hispanic Professional Engineers Award for Professional Achievement and became a member of the American Society of Mechanical Engineers that same year.

DAVID O. CRAIG is currently director of IT Back Office Applications for Reliant Resources, Inc., in Houston, Texas. He is primarily responsible for development, maintenance, and operations of the Internet and Intranet applications required to support the corporate and retail groups, specifically for the unregulated environment. Prior to joining Reliant in February 2000, Craig was with Compaq Computer Corporation. During his two years there, he was a manager in the Advanced Engineering Group where he was responsible for the design and implementation of the systems and automated equipment required to manufacture and test an advanced digital data monitor. Craig was also responsible for the patent portfolio development and prosecution and for the intellectual property strategy and operations sections of the business plan. Craig was a staff software engineer with IBM Corporation for over nine years, where his expertise was in the development of custom real-time control systems, manufacturing execution systems, and automated manufacturing systems for Fortune 500 companies. In 1996 he received the Outstanding Young Manufacturing Engineer Award and participated in the Frontiers of Engineering symposia of the National Academy of Engineering in Irvine, California, and Bremen, Germany. Craig has served on the Society of Manufacturing Engineers Education Foundation Committee for four years and as a Society of Manufacturing Engineers chapter chairman for two years. Craig holds two B.S. degrees from the Texas A&M Dwight Look College of Engineering and an M.S. from the University of Texas at Austin, where he received the George Kozmetsky Award. He holds three U.S. patents, has coauthored 11 publications in IBM's Technical Disclosure Bulletin, and was recognized with a First Level Invention Award.

JOSÉ B. CRUZ, JR., is the Howard D. Winbigler Chair in Engineering and a professor of electrical engineering at Ohio State University. From 1992 to 1997 he served as dean of engineering at Ohio State. He is also secretary of the Section on Engineering for the American Association for the Advancement of Science. Cruz was elected a member of the National Academy of Engineering (NAE) in 1980. He received the Richard E. Bellman Control Heritage Award from the American Automatic Control Council in 1994 and is a fellow of the Institute of Electrical and Electronics Engineers, elected in 1968. As a member of the NAE, Cruz currently serves on the Peer Committee on Electronics Engineering and served on the Committee on Diversity in the Engineering Workforce from 1999 to 2002 and the Academic Advisory Board from 1994 to 1997. Cruz has published several articles in scholarly journals and has edited and coauthored numerous books about electrical engineering. Cruz received his Ph.D. in electrical engineering from the University of Illinois, Urbana, his S.M. in electrical engineering from the Massachusetts Institute of Technology, and his B.S. in electrical engineering, summa cum laude, from the University of the Philippines.

PEGGY GIRSHMAN has been a broadcast journalist for 26 years. She spent her formative years working as a segment and show producer for commercial stations in Washington, D.C., and as a senior producer for several PBS series, including Scientific American Frontiers and a 26-part series on statistics. She had several positions as an editor at National Public Radio (NPR) in science and domestic news and as deputy managing editor. She was part of three start-up operations: Satellite News Channel, Monitor News Channel (Christian Science Monitor), and Video News International (a *New York Times* company attempting to pioneer the use of small-format video journalism). She has had two journalism fellowships, one at the Marine Biological Lab, the other at MIT. She was a senior medical/science producer at Dateline NBC and is now back at NPR News as an assistant managing editor. She is the winner of a national Emmy award, four local Emmy awards, and two Peabody awards for covering health care and is a cowinner of a science-writing prize from the American Association for the Advancement of Science. She serves on the board of the National Association of Science Writers and on the Journalism Fellowship for Child and Family Policy and has helped select journalists for the Knight Science Journalism Fellowship at MIT.

DANIEL E. HASTINGS is currently a professor of aeronautics and astronautics and engineering systems at the Massachusetts Institute of Technology (MIT). He is also director of MIT's Technology and Policy Program and associate director of the Engineering Systems Division. He served as chief scientist of the Air Force from 1997 to 1999. In that role he served as chief scientific adviser to the chief of staff and the secretary and provided assessments on a wide range of scientific and technical issues affecting the Air Force mission. He led several influential studies on where the Air Force should invest in space, global energy projection, and options for a science and technology workforce for the

21st century. He received a Ph.D. in aeronautics and astronautics in 1980 from MIT. From 1980 to 1985 he worked for Physical Sciences, Inc., and Oak Ridge National Laboratory in the fields of laser-material interactions and fusion plasma physics. In 1985 he joined the aeronautics and astronautics faculty at MIT as an assistant professor. His research has concentrated on issues related to spacecraft-environmental inter-actions, space propulsion, space systems engineering, and space policy. He has published many papers and a book on spacecraft-environment interactions and several papers on space propulsion and space systems. He has taught courses and seminars in plasma physics, rocket propul-sion, advanced space power and propulsion systems, aerospace policy, and space systems engineering. His recent research has concentrated on issues of space systems and space policy. He is a fellow of the American Institute of Aeronautics and Astronautics and a member of the Inter-national Academy of Astronautics. He serves as a member of the National Aeronautics and Space Administration Advisory Council and the National Academies Government-University-Industry Research Roundtable and is chair of the Applied Physics Lab Science and Tech-nology Advisory Panel as well as the Air Force Scientific Advisory Board. He is a member of the MIT Lincoln Laboratory Advisory Committee and is on the board of trustees of the Aerospace Corporation. He also served as a member of the National Academy of Engineering's 1996 and 1997 Organizing Committee for the Frontiers of Engineering sympo-sium. He is a consultant to the Institute for Defense Analysis.

MICHAEL J. HELLER is a founder of Nanogen, Inc., and has served as its chief technical officer since September 1993. In November 1991, Dr. Heller cofounded Nanogen's former parent company, Nanotronics, and since that time has served as vice president of research. He co-founded and served as president and chief operating officer of Integrated DNA Technologies from 1987 to 1989 and from 1984 to 1987 served as director of molecular biology for Molecular Biosystems, Inc. Prior to 1984 he served as supervisor of DNA Technology and Molecular Biology for Standard Oil Company. Dr. Heller received a Ph.D. in bio-chemistry from Colorado State University.

DEBORAH G. JOHNSON is the Anne Shirley Carter Olsson Professor of Applied Ethics, Division of Technology, Culture, and Communica-tion, School of Engineering and Applied Science at the University of

Virginia. She is the author/editor of four books: *Computer Ethics* (now in its third edition; Prentice Hall, 2001), *Computers, Ethic and Social Values* (coedited with Helen Nissenbaum; Prentice Hall, 1995), *Ethical Issues in Engineering* (Prentice Hall, 1991), and *Ethical Issues in the Use of Computers* (coedited with John Snapper; Wadsworth Publishing Co., 1985) and dozens of articles focusing on engineering and computer ethics and technology policy. Active in professional organizations, Professor Johnson has served as president of the Society for Philosophy and Technology, treasurer of the Association for Computing Machinery (ACM) Special Interest Group on Computers and Society (SIGCAS), and chair of the American Philosophical Association Committee on Computer Use in Philosophy. Currently, she serves as president of a new professional society, the International Society for Ethics and Information Technology. In 2000 Professor Johnson received the ACM SIGCAS Making a Difference Award, and in 2001 she received the American Society for Engineering Education Sterling Olmsted Award for "innovative contributions to liberal education within engineering education."

ALAN C. KAY is a senior fellow at Hewlett-Packard Laboratories and founder and president of Viewpoints Research Institute, Inc., best known for the ideas of personal computing, the intimate laptop computer, and the inventions of the now ubiquitous overlapping-window interface and modern object-oriented programming. His deep interests in children and education were the catalysts for these ideas, and they continue to be a source of inspiration to him. One of the founders of the Xerox Palo Alto Research Center (PARC), he led one of the several groups that together developed modern workstations (and the forerunners of the Macintosh), Smalltalk, the overlapping-window interface, Desktop Publishing, the Ethernet, Laser printing, and network "client-servers." Prior to his work at Xerox, Dr. Kay was a member of the University of Utah Advanced Research Projects Agency research team that developed three-dimensional graphics. There he earned a doctorate (with distinction) in 1969 for developing of the first graphical object-oriented personal computer. He holds undergraduate degrees in mathematics and molecular biology from the University of Colorado and master of science and doctoral degrees in computer science from the University of Utah. Kay also participated in the original design of the ARPANet, which later became the Internet. After Xerox PARC, Kay was chief scientist of Atari, a fellow at Apple Computer for 12 years, and then for 5 years vice president of research and development at the Walt Disney Company. He then founded Viewpoints Research Institute in 2001. Dr. Kay has received numerous honors, including the Association for Computing Machinery (ACM) Software Systems Award, the ACM Outstanding Educator Award, the J-D Warnier Prix D'Informatique, and the NEC 2001 C&C Prize. He has been elected a fellow of the American Academy of Arts and Sciences, the Royal Society of Arts, and the Computer Museum History Center and is a member of the National Academy of Engineering. He recently received the ZeroOne Award from the University of Berlin and the National Academy of Engineering's prestigious Charles Stark Draper Prize for his contributions to the development of the world's first practical networked personal computers. A former professional jazz guitarist, composer, and theatrical designer, he is now an amateur classical pipe organist.

TAREK M. KHALIL received his Ph.D. and M.S. in industrial engineering from Texas Tech University and his B.S. in mechanical engineering from Cairo University. He is a professor of industrial engineering at the University of Miami and holds professorships in biomedical engineering, epidemiology and public health, and neurological surgery. He served as chairman of the University of Miami Department of Industrial Engineering and as dean of the University of Miami Graduate School. He is a registered professional engineer in the state of Florida. Dr. Khalil is the founder and current president of the International Association for Management of Technology and regional vice president of Alpha Pi Mu. He served the Institute of Industrial Engineers (IIE) as chairman of the Council of Fellows, director of the Work Measurement and Methods Engineering Division, vice president of Region IV, member of the Board of Trustees, and president of the Miami Chapter. Dr. Khalil is the recipient of many awards, including the Award for Technical Innovation in Industrial Engineering; Doctor Honoris Causa from the Institut National Polytechnique de Loraine, France; the University of Miami College of Engineering Researcher of the Year Award; the IIE Phil Carroll Award; the David F. Baker Award; the IIE Ergonomics Division Award; the Human Factors Society Paul M. Fitts Award; and the Jack A. Craft Award. He is a member of Alpha Pi Mu, Alpha Epsilon Lambda, Tau Beta Pi, Omicron Delta Kappa, Sigma Xi,

Phi Kappa Phi, and many professional organizations. He is the author of more than 300 publications and many books.

ROBERT W. LUCKY is a frequent columnist for *IEEE Spectrum*, discussing future scenarios of electrical engineers. Dr. Lucky previously appeared on Bill Moyers's show, "A World of Ideas," where he discussed the impacts of future technological advances. He is the author of the popular book *Silicon Dreams* (St. Martin's Press, 1989), which is a semitechnical and philosophical discussion of the ways in which both humans and computers deal with information. Dr. Lucky attended Purdue University, where he received a B.S. degree in electrical engineering in 1957 and M.S. and Ph.D. degrees in 1959 and 1961, respectively. After graduation he joined AT&T Bell Laboratories, where he was initially involved in studying ways of sending digital information over telephone lines. The best-known outcome of this work was his invention of the adaptive equalizer—a technique for correcting distortion in telephone signals that is used in all high-speed data transmissions today. The textbook on data communications that he coauthored became the most cited reference in the communications field over the period of a decade. At Bell Labs he became executive director of the Communications Sciences Research Division in 1982, where he was responsible for research on the methods and technologies for future communications systems. In 1992 he assumed his present position at Telcordia. He has been active in professional activities and has served as president of the Communications Society of the Institute of Electrical and Electronics Engineers (IEEE) and as vice president and executive vice president of the parent IEEE itself. He has been editor of several technical journals, including the *Proceedings of the IEEE*, and since 1982 has written the bimonthly "Reflections" column of personalized observations about the engineering profession for *Spectrum* magazine. A collection of the articles appear in the book, *Lucky Strikes . . . Again* (IEEE Press, 1993).

JOHN M. MULVEY is professor of operations research and financial engineering in the School of Engineering and Applied Science at Princeton University. He is a leading expert in large-scale optimization models and algorithms, especially financial applications. He has implemented integrated risk management for many large companies, including American Express, Towers Perrin–Tillinghast, Pacific Mutual, St. Paul Insurance, and Siemens Financial Services. These systems link the key risks within the organization and assist the company in making high-level decisions. In addition, he has built significant planning systems for government agencies, including the Office of Tax Analysis for the Treasury Department, the Joint Chiefs of Staff in the Defense Department, and personal planning for the U.S. Army. He has edited four books and published over 100 scholarly papers.

SHARON L. NUNES is currently director of life sciences solutions at IBM, responsible for bringing new technology solutions to the pharmaceutical and biotech markets. She was previously director of technology evaluation, responsible for corporate-wide emerging technologies activities. She has held many management positions at IBM, ranging from research to development and manufacturing, as well as positions in hardware development, software development, and networking. Nunes spent 14 years in IBM research and was responsible for the launch of IBM's Computational Biology Center in 1997. This worldwide research organization was a key driver in highlighting IBM's business opportunities in the life sciences market. Nunes received her Ph.D. in materials science in 1983 from the University of Connecticut. She is a member of the Advisory Council of the Whitaker Biomedical Engineering Institute at Johns Hopkins University, a member of the Board of Governors of the Mathematical Sciences Institute at Ohio State University, a member of the Board of Governors of the Advanced Physics Laboratory at Johns Hopkins University, and a member of the Board of Directors of the Single Nucleotide Polymorphisms (SNP) Consortium. She was a National Academy of Engineering "Frontiers of Engineering" fellow in 2000.

HENRY PETROSKI is the Aleksandar S. Vesic Professor of Civil Engineering and a professor of history at Duke University. He has written on many aspects of engineering and technology, including design, success and failure, error and judgment, the history of engineering and technology, and the use of case studies in education and practice. His books include: *To Engineer Is Human* (St. Martin's Press, 1985), *The Pencil* (Knopf, 1990), *The Evolution of Useful Things* (Knopf, 1992), *Design Paradigms* (Cambridge University Press, 1994), *Engineers of Dreams* (Knopf, 1995), *Remaking the World* (Knopf, 1997), *Invention by Design*

(Harvard University Press, 1998), *The Book on the Bookshelf* (Knopf, 1999), and *Paperboy* (Knopf, 2002), a memoir about the influences that led him to become an engineer. In addition to having published the usual technical articles in the refereed journals of applied mechanics, Petroski has published numerous articles and essays in newspapers and magazines, including the *New York Times, Washington Post,* and *Wall Street Journal.* Since 1991 he has written the engineering column in the bimonthly magazine *American Scientist* and since 2000 has written a column on the engineering profession for *ASEE Prism.* He lectures regularly in the United States and abroad and has been interviewed frequently on radio and television. Petroski is a professional engineer registered in Texas. He has been a Guggenheim fellow, a National Endowment for the Humanities fellow, and a National Humanities Center fellow. Among his other honors are the Ralph Coats Roe Medal from the American Society of Mechanical Engineers; the Civil Engineering History and Heritage Award from the American Society of Civil Engineers; honorary degrees from Clarkson University, Trinity College (Hartford, Conn.), and Valparaiso University; and distinguished engineering alumnus awards from Manhattan College and the University of Illinois at Urbana-Champaign. He is a fellow of the American Society of Civil Engineers and the Institution of Engineers of Ireland, an honorary member of the Moles, and a member of the National Academy of Engineering.

SUE V. ROSSER has served as dean of Ivan Allen College, the liberal arts college at Georgia Tech, where she is also a professor of history, technology, and society, since July 1999. From July 1995 to July 1999, Dr. Rosser served as professor of anthropology at the University of Florida. She also directed the Center for Women's Studies and Gender Research. From July 1994 to December 1995 she was senior program officer for women's programs at the National Science Foundation. From 1986 to 1995 she served as director of women's studies at the University of South Carolina, where she also was a professor of family and preventive medicine at the medical school. Dr. Rosser has researched and published extensively on topics related to women in science fields. Her most recent book is *Re-Engineering Female Friendly Science* (Teachers College Press, 1997). She currently serves on the editorial boards of the *National Women's Studies Association Journal* and *Women's Studies Quarterly.* Dr. Rosser received her undergraduate, master's, and doctoral degrees in zoology from the University of Wisconsin, Madison.

ERNEST T. SMERDON, after three years as senior education associate at the National Science Foundation, is dean emeritus at the University of Arizona. He was vice provost and dean of the College of Engineering there from 1988 to 1998. Earlier he held the Janet S. Cockrell Centennial Chair in the Department of Civil Engineering at the University of Texas at Austin and prior to that the Bess Harris Jones Centennial Professorship in Natural Resource Policy Studies at the LBJ School of Public Affairs. From 1976 until 1982 he was vice chancellor for academic affairs for the University of Texas system. Dr. Smerdon has been president of the American Society for Engineering Education and chair of its Engineering Deans Council. He was elected to the National Academy of Engineering (NAE) in 1986. He has served on seven NAE committees including as chair of its Committee on Career-Long Education for Engineers, as a member of its Academic Advisory Board, and the Committee on the Technology Policy Options in a Global Economy. He has served on 11 National Research Council committees and chaired two. He was a board member of the Accreditation Board for Engineering and Technology and represented the board on the Engineering Accreditation Commission. He received the highest honor of the American Society of Civil Engineers when he was elected an honorary member in 1994. Other society honors include awards from the American Society of Civil Engineers, the American Society of Agricultural Engineers, and the American Water Resources Association. His alma mater, the University of Missouri, Columbia, chose him for the Honor Award for Distinguished Service in Engineering and in December 2003 awarded him an honorary degree, doctor of science, honoris causa. He was program cochair for an international colloquium on engineering education in Berlin sponsored by the American Society for Engineering Education, the European Society for Engineering Education, and the Berlin Technical University. He has written widely on engineering education and has spoken on the subject in 12 countries outside the United States. He now spends most of his time on engineering education issues.

PROJECT LIAISON

STEPHEN W. DIRECTOR is Robert J. Vlasic Dean of Engineering and professor of electrical engineering and computer science at the University of Michigan. He received a B.S. degree from the State University of New York at Stony Brook in 1965 and his M.S. and Ph.D. degrees in electrical engineering from the University of California, Berkeley, in 1967 and 1968, respectively. From 1968 until 1977 he was with the Department of Electrical Engineering at the University of Florida, Gainesville. He joined Carnegie Mellon University in 1977, where he was Helen Whitaker University Professor of Electrical and Computer Engineering, head of the Department of Electrical and Computer Engineering from 1982 to 1991, and then dean of the College of Engineering until June 1996. Dr. Director is a pioneer in the area of computer-aided design and has a long record of commitment to and innovation in engineering education, including authoring pioneering textbooks and motivating and implementing new and innovative electrical and computer engineering curricula. He has published over 150 papers and authored or coauthored six texts. He currently serves as chair of the National Academy of Engineering (NAE) Committee on Engineering Education and as chair of the Board of Directors of the American Society for Engineering Education Engineering Deans Council. He chaired the former NAE Academic Advisory Board. He also serves on numerous other boards and committees and as a consultant to industry and academia. Dr. Director has received many awards for his research and educational contributions, including the 1998 Institute of Electrical and Electronics Engineers (IEEE) Education Medal and the 1999 Distinguished Engineering Alumnus Award from the University of California, Berkeley. Dr. Director is a fellow of the IEEE and a member of the NAE.